C000138071

KIDW

Memories of

Kidwelly Castle.

PBQB

Sponsored by

GRAVELLS

founded in Kidwelly by
T. B. Gravell, M.B.E., in 1932

Kidwelly Castle & St Marys Church.

KIDWELLY

Memories of Yesteryear

by

ERIC HUGHES

Sketches/Line Drawings:
PETER BURT

Published by the Author

First Impression 2003

Copyright © Eric Hughes 2003

Published by Eric Hughes
Cheriton, Greenfield, Kidwelly
Carmarthenshire, SA17 4PS
Telephone: (01554) 890312

*All rights reserved. No part of this publication may
be reproduced, stored in a retrieval system,
or transmitted, in any form or by any means,
electronic, mechanical, photocopying, recording,
or otherwise, without the prior
permission of the publisher.*

ISBN 0 9537478 1 6

*Printed in Wales by
Dinefwr Press
Rawlings Road, Llandybïe
Carmarthenshire, SA18 3YD*

Contents

ACKNOWLEDGEMENTS 6

FOREWORD 7

INTRODUCTION 9

1. S.S. *PAUL* OF HAMBURG 11

2. TRIUMPHS AND DISASTERS 20

3. SPORT AND ENTERTAINMENT 37

4. ARSENIC POISONING TRIAL 48

5. NOTABLE EVENTS 79

6. UNUSUAL OCCURRENCES AND ODDITIES 90

7. WAR MEMORIAL 97

8. KIDWELLY MURDER TRIAL 104

9. LOCAL CORONATION CELEBRATIONS 131

10. RELIGION 143

11. PEOPLE AND PLACES 159

12. HORSE RACING DYNASTY 168

BIBLIOGRAPHY 176

Acknowledgements

In our busy world, time is precious and we never seem to have enough, yet the following people gave generously of theirs and I cannot thank them enough for their help in the preparation of this book.

Mrs Mary Williams for patiently typing and retyping the manuscript and for enhancing the text. Mr Peter Burt whose excellent illustrations have brought the book to life. Dr Terry James for writing the 'Foreword' and for good advice. Mr Douglas Davies for reading the proofs and for his encouragement.

Mr Neville Jones, Mrs Mair Morgan, Mr T. B. Gravell, Mr Selwyn Edwards, Mr Oliver Colwill, Miss Mair Rowlands, Mrs Mair Protheroe, Mr Eric Williams, Mrs Iris Davies, Mrs Janice Rowlands, Mrs Catherine Francis, Rev. Richard Jenkins, Mr Jack Lewis and Mr Denzil Morris.

The very helpful staff at Carmarthen Borough Library, Llanelli Town Library and Carmarthen Record Office.

To Messrs Emyr Nicholas and Eddie John and all the staff at Dinefwr Press for their guidance and support and great care in the final production of this book.

Last, but by no means least, my wife Margaret for her support, patience and encouragement throughout.

Foreword

I feel that this book has a twofold purpose:

Firstly, to make a permanent record of the many stories, legends and facts about Kidwelly lest, over the years, they vanish and are forgotten. Secondly, that Kidwelly has a history not only of stone and mortar but of human trials and tribulations, joy and sadness and of immense human endeavour.

To paraphrase Saunders Lewis when writing of Wales in general, I have particularised it – "A vineyard in our care is *Kidwelly* – it is important to deliver to our children, intact, an eternal heritage." We are living in an era of globalization; digital technology's dizzying capacity to shuffle, combine, alter and duplicate images; of the new world of CD Rom, or virtual reality, of cyberspace and the internet. It is, therefore, more important than ever that we do not lose sight of our local history, without falling into the dangers of parochialism, insularity or xenophobia.

This book will serve to inform and remind us of our past and present. It is the result of much research, unravelling and sifting of material. Needless to say, it is far from complete; however, let us hope that it will be an incentive to the author to delve still further into the fruit-laden vineyard of Kidwelly, old and new.

Diolch yn fawr, Eric.

Dr. Terry James

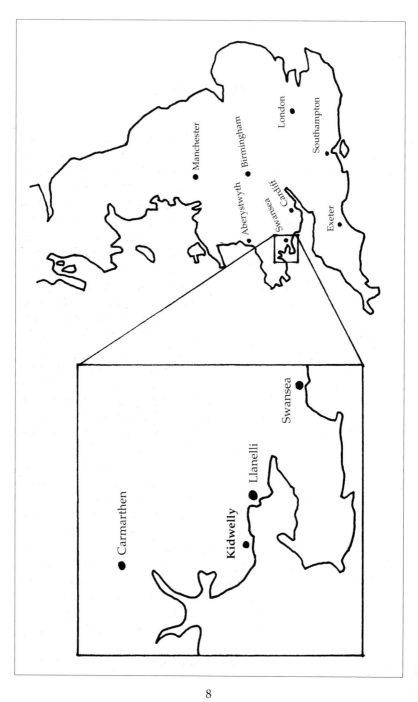

Introduction

This publication is an update and follow-on of my previous book which was entitled *History of Kidwelly*. I have concentrated on the last two centuries to reveal events, people and places which were of great interest to me and I am sure will appeal to the reader.

Born and bred in the town, I have unfolded tales which have fascinated me since childhood. I recall looking with awe at the immense hulk of the weathered disintegrating shipwrecked 'Paul'. I have recorded the enjoyment and celebrations of the Coronation week in 1953 and the excitement and phenomenal live television pictures of the event. I have unfolded dark tales of 'goings on' at Rumsey House, the home of solicitor Harold Greenwood. I have recounted the joys and excitement of the annual visits of St Luke's Fair, with the park and all neighbouring streets crowded with stalls, and the most enjoyable twice-a-week visits to the Kidwelly Cinema.

In addition, during my researches I have unearthed some gems relating to incidents which have occurred in the town, such as the capture of a monster fish near the town bridge, the case of the missing railway fireman thrust from the tender of a high speed train, the removal of a farm by rail from Kidwelly to Buckinghamshire. The moving ceremony at the unveiling of the War Memorial by a mother who had lost three of her sons in the conflict. The emotional murder trial relating to a young boy aged 11 found buried near Stockwell where a mother and her two sons were charged with his murder.

I have also spotlighted historic occasions such as the first Welsh borough to receive the power of self government; the construction of the second tinplate works in Britain; opening of the first canal to be established in Wales; widening of the mediaeval town bridge; the first carnival in the town; the knighthood of Sir Alfred Stephens; the local lad who won the Grand National three times; installation of 'Welcome' signs at points of entry into the town; initial illumination of the town clock; election of the first female mayor, and a royal visit by Prince Charles.

I have exposed sadness at the closure of the ROF Factory at Pembrey and the Optical Factory at Greenfields, which contrasted so much with the joys of recalling famous sporting successes and notable musical achievements.

I believe I have identified life as it was in our small historical town and I trust you enjoy it.

1.

s.s. *Paul* of Hamburg

On October 29th, 1925, a four-masted schooner, the s.s. *Paul* of Hamburg, ran aground at Cefn Sidan sands, the last sailing ship to be wrecked on this perilous stretch in the estuary. The crew of sixteen which included one woman, suffered an alarming experience in heavy ponderous seas, preceding rescue by the Ferryside Lifeboat.

For over threequarters of a century, substantial timbers of the wrecked schooner could be seen off the shoreline near to the seashore known to the locals as the 'Bertwn'. By the Spring of 2002 the wreck was out of sight, the result of constantly shifting sands, and no trace can at present be seen. However, sand movements do take place here, especially during stormy weather and the wreck could possibly be exposed again. The *Paul* was a local landmark during the time I was growing up and there is a missing link now it is no longer to be seen. The 'Bertwn' is Kidwelly's local beach, located just 1½ miles away and for youngsters it was quite a challenge to walk out to the wreck at low tide.

s.s. Paul *aground on Cefn Sidan sands.*
(Photograph courtesy Peter Evans).

11

s.s. Paul, *1925. Stranded on the sandbank.*
(Photograph: Author).

s.s. Paul. *Morning after the disaster.*
(Photograph courtesy Peter Evans).

DREADED CEFN SIDAN – GERMAN CREW'S PERIL

In the early hours of that Friday morning, the four-masted sailing ship the s.s. *Paul* of Hamburg ran aground at Cefn Sidan sands, a well-known danger spot. The schooner was under the command of Capt. Hans Blade.

The s.s. *Paul* was a wooden schooner, of 1,538 tons gross, carrying a cargo of about 2,000 tons of timber on a voyage from Halifax, Nova Scotia, off the east coast of Canada, to the port at Milford Haven in West Wales. Drifting onto the much dreaded Cefn Sidan sands (scene of a good number of wrecks of past years) during a violent storm and thick fog, was the climax to a series of exceptionally troublesome events in the latter stages of its 27-day passage. The schooner had battled against rough weather and heavy seas for the previous nine days or so, had lost some of her sails and failed to negotiate St Anne's Head. At 3.30 a.m. on Friday, October 29th, she was driven into Carmarthen Bay and onto the notorious Cefn Sidan sands.

The crew launched distress flares soon after midnight and distress flags were raised in daylight hours. Immediately the fog lifted, the vessel could be seen from Ferryside and the alarm was raised when the ship's obvious perilous position was exposed. The lifeboat crew was summoned instantly, and in no time the boat *Richard Ashley*, with coxwain David Jones in command, was ploughing through a heavy menacing sea to effect a rescue. The vessel had run aground at a point six miles from the Ferryside Lifeboat Station and as the rescue craft drew near, it became clear that members of the schooner had already launched their own lifeboat in an attempt to reach the shore. However, due to the strength of the ebbing tide, the schooner's lifeboat with eleven crew (including one female) was already a mile distant from the stranded schooner, and drifting out to Carmarthen Bay. The coxwain quickly identified the seriousness of the situation and changed course to pursue the schooner's craft which by then was filling with water and threatening to swamp. With great difficulty the twice jeopardised seamen were frantically transferred to the *Richard Ashley* which then returned to the stricken vessel. The crew showed tremendous courage as they battled against the heavy seas to take on board the remaining five stranded mariners, including the captain.

The brave lifeboatmen had worked with great energy and courage; all 16 members of the *Paul* (owner of the boat and the stewardess included) were saved. The rescue operations lasted over four hours, watched anxiously by a large crowd gathered on shore, who cheered enthusiastically both rescued and rescuers when the lifeboat returned to terra firma. Every participant in the rescue was taken to the local White Lion Hotel, where they were given all possible attention. Some injuries had been sustained but these were quickly attended to by Dr D. Lewis Williams.

Col. R. A. Neville of 'Undercliffe', Ferryside, was secretary of the Lifeboat Institution and during the morning had supervised the rescue operations. He spoke warmly of the prompt and heroic efforts of the coxwain and his crew, who were without any doubt responsible for saving the lives of the *Paul*'s personnel.

Survivors of the s.s. Paul.
(Photograph courtesy Peter Evans).

Under the command of Capt. Hans Bade, the *Paul's* anchor had dragged a considerable distance, eventually coming to grief on the hostile sandbank.

Capt. David Jones had been coxwain at Ferryside for 34 years and he praised the gallant efforts of his crew. The *Richard Ashley* had replaced an older lifeboat – the *City of Manchester*. On July 20th, 1920, the s.s. *Cadir* of Bilbao had issued distress signals, and on its last day of service the *City of Manchester* had assisted and stood by the displaced vessel until she was out of danger.

The following vessels are former wreck victims of the insidious Cefn Sidan sands: *Teviotdale* in 1886 – 11 lives saved, seventeen lost. The s.s. *Craiguhine* in 1899, when the whole crew of 22 were rescued. The s.s. *Australia* in 1901 – 15 members of the crew saved, 2 killed through a collapse of the mast and rigging. In March 1905 the *City of Manchester* lifeboat also stood by and assisted the s.s. *Signe*, the vessel ultimately being taken to Burry Port.

Hans Bade, Captain of the s.s. *Paul*, had good knowledge of the English language, and when interviewed by a local newspaper he gave an account of the events in a calm and simple manner. He said: "The *Paul* left Halifax, Nova Scotia, with a cargo of timber for house building. The vessel had called in Queenstown and was making for St Anne's Head in Pembrokeshire. In Carmarthen Bay on Thursday night we went into thick fog and a gale sprung up. Some of our sails were blown away and others 'dragged', and we drifted onto the sands. We hoisted distress signals early on Friday morning and the lifeboat came to take us off some hours later."

The Captain spoke well of the Ferryside people who had been so kind to him and his crew. "After we had all got on the lifeboat," added the captain, "one of the apprentices, Adolf Radaei, youngest member of the crew, remembered we had left the ship's canary on the vessel, so he climbed the rope ladder to fetch her. The bird is now safe and sound."

"Adolf Radaei," he added, "by the way, celebrated his 15th birthday on the day of the wreck."

One of the crew of the *Paul* was Hans Sager of Flemisberg, who was the owner and was signed on as paymaster. All were Germans with two exceptions – the Canadian stewardess, Pearl May Asch of New Glasgow, Nova Scotia (a half caste), and the cook, Svenning Nielsen of Uloberg, Denmark.

The Shipwrecked Mariners Society financially supported the stranded crew for the first 24 hours, after which the Cardiff-based

German Consul in Wales took over responsibility for their care. He visited Ferryside on Saturday, October 30th, and made arrangements for the crew to leave on the following Wednesday.

The rescued crew were well looked after when they landed at Ferryside. Mrs Susan Thomas, wife of one of the lifeboatmen, took in the stewardess and Mr Brigstocke, Roberts Rest, generously put up 10 of the men. The remainder were accommodated at the White Lion Hotel, where the licensee, Mr H. M. Bright, made them most welcome. All the men had their meals at the White Lion Hotel.

Most of the crew attended divine service at St Thomas's Church on the Sunday morning and the hymn 'For those in peril on the sea' was sung by the congregation during the service. On the Monday evening an impromptu dance was arranged by the villagers, as a farewell party for the visitors and locals who had experienced such perils in the previous few days. Nearly all the crew attended and enjoyed a pleasant evening and paid tribute to the splendid care given them in Ferryside.

Following on after the rescue the weather was even worse and a strong tide drove the schooner further ashore, close to the remains of *Teviotdale*, a wreck of a previous crisis. In an attempt to save the *Paul*, Cardiff tug *Beaver* with Lieut. D. J. Raver in command arrived on Saturday afternoon, but because of the heavy ground sea running at the time, operations were postponed until Sunday morning's tide. The tug put out to sea early next morning but again the weather was boisterous and efforts to get near the wreck were negative. The prospects in the evening were no better and even on Monday morning a further postponement, as conditions were if anything worse than ever they had been since the arrival of the tug. Supervising the operations on the Saturday were – Mr A. Matthews (German Embassy) with his surveyor Mr J. Wilson and Commander G. J. Wheeler who represented underwriters for the cargo.

On Monday morning Mr Coombes (Messrs Coombes & Co., Ship-brokers based in Llanelly), agent for Lloyd's in this district, and a representative of a Liverpool salvage firm, decided on an attempt to retrieve the deck cargo, the work to be supervised by Mr Charles Thomas, Warwick House, Ferryside, sub-agent for Lloyd's. The approximate weight of this part of the cargo was 500 tons, and a bid would be made to complete the work in about 7-10 days. Some doubt was cast on the time-scale as conditions were none too favourable. The task was begun on Tuesday morning when a gang of 28 men, mostly local fishermen, showed up to start work on the project. It was

Mr Harry Jones and son, Neville, on the wreck of the s.s. Paul. *Summer 1949.*
(Photograph courtesy Neville Jones).

proposed to 'raft' the timber and tow it across to the Bertwn, a well-known local landmark located between Ferryside and Kidwelly, close to the GWR main railway line, where it would be stacked ready for removal.

When these arrangements had been made, the *Beaver* left Ferryside heading for Cardiff on Tuesday's morning tide. Further endeavours

Wreck of the s.s. Paul, *1975.*
Note: St Ishmael's Holiday Village in the background.
(Photograph courtesy Peter Evans).

were now impossible due to the prevailing falling tides but the tug was expected to return on the following Monday.

The s.s. *Paul* lay stranded on the sandbank like an enormous whale and conditions for recovery of the cargo deteriorated further. The cargo of timber was partly stored on deck and the lashing holding the timber in place had now broken away.

The *Beaver* returned and again made several attempts to dislodge the grounded vessel. Other tugs also tried but they too were not able to tow the schooner off the sandbank. The *Paul* by now had suffered a broken keel, and being constructed of wood, the seams opened up on both sides, spilling out in a large amount of the cargo.

In October of the following year, Lloyd's agent announced that she had been disposed of and was now a wreck.

Her career had been brief. She was built in America in 1919 by the Macateer Shipbuilding Company of Seattle, her owners were Norwegian who named her *Mount Whitney*. She was 1,538 tons gross, 1,367 net; she measured 230 feet long, 45 feet wide and 18 feet deep. The designation of her rig was that of a four-masted fore-and-aft schooner, a pattern favoured by the Americans who toward the end of the 1914-1918 war, built a number of these wood vessels to conserve stocks of steel. In 1924, her new owner named her *Margaretha Sager* and the following year the name was changed to *Paul*, her port of registry was Hamburg.

One of the methods used in salvage attempts was to fill the ship with watertight casks which were netted down. When the tide came in the plan went awry as the casks burst through the nets instead of lifting the vessel. The casks floated away in the direction of Kidwelly and word soon got out that the Gwendraeth Fach river, just below the town bridge, was awash with new 45-gallon barrels. Many of the houses in Station Road which runs alongside the river, were soon sporting brand new water butts.

Another local tale is that of an inventive Kidwelly character who stowed himself in the wreckage shortly before the tide came in. When the police guard were driven back to the beach by the tide, he was able to prepare a huge bundle of anything that could float. He lashed it together with a rope and jumped over the side with his bundle. The incoming tide carried him and his booty all the way to Kidwelly town bridge.

The main photograph shows clearly the vessel s.s. *Paul* to be a four-masted schooner. However, shortly after the wrecking, one mast was sawn off and spirited away in the dead of night. Later photographs of the wreck will confirm the act of theft as they show the ship having only three masts.

The Burry estuary, especially the treacherous Cefn Sidan sands, forms a graveyard of many vessels shipwrecked by fog, unmarked river channels, shifting sandbanks and gales. The most frequent reason for these accidents was neglect by the captains to take soundings in good time. Sailors were deceived by the vast expanse of water and failed to appreciate how shallow it was. Passing vessels, not heading for the Burry estuary were often driven into it, only to end up as wrecks.

When shipping started to use the estuary regularly, charts and maps were essential for safety purposes, and dreaded areas such as Cefn Sidan were then clearly defined.

In these days of modern steering controls, ships are less likely to be blown off course, as happened to the s.s. *Paul* of Hamburg. But Cefn Sidan continues to be one of the most hazardous sites and is listed on countless dangerous water registers throughout the world.

2

Triumphs and Disasters

TRIUMPHS

1444 – Self Government

A Charter granted by Henry VI was a significant development in the history of the town as it gave extensive powers of self government. It brought into existence the Corporation of Kidwelly, the title of Mayor, bailiffs and aldermen of the town. It was the first of the Welsh boroughs to receive this important principle of incorporation embodied in a charter. The mayor is lord, holding court in the town, and the very first holder of the title 'Mayor of the Borough of Kidwelly' was John Aylward.

August 1737 – Second in Britain

Charles Gwyn of Kidwelly, Tinman, erected a rolling mill, and other relevant conveniences to a tin works, on the banks of the Gwendraeth Fach located one mile north of the town. This tin works established in 1737 was the second earliest in Britain, Pontypool being the first.

1766 – First in Wales

In the year 1766 Thomas Kymer built the first canal in Wales. The canal conducive to industry ran from Kymer's colliery at Great Forest, Carway, to the quayside at Kidwelly, measuring a distance of three miles.

April 1877 – Foundation Stone

A foundation stone for a new Town Hall was laid by Mrs Evans, wife of the town mayor Ald. T. W. A. Evans of Rumsey House. Mr Thomas of The Cottage, stated that "the old town hall was built in 1632, almost 250 years ago, was an adornment being the only slated roof building in the borough for many years." Mr W. G. Williams of Burry Port was the contractor who undertook construction of the hall.

October 1877 – Preliminary Opening of the New Town Hall

Visitors to the ancient borough of Kidwelly were dismayed at the dilapidated condition of the old Town Hall. It was demolished and in a very short space of time replaced by a Gothic structure. The official opening of the new Guildhall took place even though there was still some work outstanding inside the building. Introductory ringing of the new hall bells which hung in the turret heralded commencement of proceedings and a Union Jack flag embellished with the Borough of Kidwelly Coat of Arms flew high and proud above the brand new building. When official ceremonies were over, the distinguished guests who had honoured the occasion formed a procession. A drum and fife band headed the parade, followed by the mace and halberd bearers, members of the police force, new mayor Ald. T. W. A. Evans and justices dressed in scarlet robes, members of the corporation and many other townspeople. The pageant made its way to Rumsey House with huge crowds on the streets to witness the special event and children of the British and National schools lined the streets as well. Later on, they came together at the new hall to mingle with notable guests, and to partake of the cake and wine served by Mrs Chappell of the Castle Inn and other helpers. In the afternoon a large contingent sat down with the mayor and his guests to dine at the Pelican Hotel.

October 1883 – Iron Horse Triumphs

At the Annual St Luke's Fair, Monday was the appointed day for the sale of cattle and on Tuesday pigs were sold with porkers fetching eleven shillings. Hand in hand with the fair came the swings, merry-go-round, shooting gallery, etc., to give exhilarating entertainment. A striking feature was Studt's massive traction engine, completely new to the area, which gave rise to great excitement. Unfortunately,

Traction Engine

when it arrived the ground was a quagmire of mud and not in a fit state to allow the engine entry into the fairfield, rendering it useless to activate the 'Sea on Land' attraction.

Mr Alexander Young, proprietor of the Mynydd-y-Garreg Lime Works and Railway, had recently taken delivery of some heavy machinery. The consignment, comprising a grinding mill, engine and boiler combined, had been dispatched from Leeds and transported to the Sidings at Mynydd-y-Garreg. It remained there on hold because of seemingly insurmountable difficulties of transporting it to the quarry. It was considered quite impractical to use horses as a mode of transport due to the unavoidable dangerously steep hills to be negotiated.

Mr Young came up with the idea that Studt's traction engine could be an ideal means of conveying the equipment to its intended quarters. The interested parties got together, came to an arrangement, and to the wonder and astonishment of the quiet inhabitants of Mynydd-y-Garreg, the iron horse with its enormous load was soon steadily and slowly rolling its way through the village. The load arrived safely, having taken four hours to reach its destination, a mere one and a quarter miles away.

For their part, the Studt brothers managed and manoeuvred their engine with amazing dexterity, to overcome the intricate sharp bends, as well as the steep, winding and hilly terrain.

March 1911 – Ely Racecourse

Ivor Anthony, native of Kidwelly and a well-known jockey, won the Welsh Grand National on his mount 'Razorbill' which took place at Ely Racecourse located near Cardiff.

1913 – Challenge Cup Winner

On August Bank Holiday in the year 1910, the newly formed Mynydd-y-Garreg Band entered their first contest which took place in Llanelly. No marks awarded, but a comment to "Go home and train." They took the advice and rehearsed twice a week. The band continued to play at various contests but despite disciplined practice the coveted prize was not for them. In 1912, however, success at last – they were placed twice, 3rd in Carmarthen at Easter time, and 2nd at Llandovery in July.

In 1913, the band finally came to its own by winning at three contests – 1st prize at Llandovery at Whitsun time, 1st prize at Kidwelly Castle in July, and first prize and challenge cup at Kidwelly Market Hall in December.

Mynydd-y-Garreg Silver Band – 1926 Tour to Tenby and Caldey Island.
Top row, left to right: George Lewis, Davey Thomas Walters, Jack Richards, Edwin Lewis, Davey Thomas Gravell.
Second row: Davey James Evans, ?, ?, Tom Evans, Phil Jones, Tommy Roberts, Johnny Roberts, Jack Harries, Dick Walters, Phil Gravell.
Third row: Phil Davies, Dan Gravell, John Ellis Roberts, David William Gravell (Conductor),
Griff Williams, Johnny Thomas, Davey Tom Gravell. Front row: Jim Gravell, Bryn Gravell, Tom Harries, Handel Williams.
(Photograph: Author).

March 1915 – Grand National Winner
Time for congratulations and celebrations in the district when the plum Grand National prize was won by a local lad. Jack Anthony, son of Mr and Mrs John Anthony of Cilfeithy Farm, won the epic race on his mount 'Ally Sloper'.

February 1944 – Wings for Victory
London's mammoth target of raising £500,000 during Wings for Victory Week was magnificently realised. Sir Harold Mackintosh, speaking to a large crowd gathered in Trafalgar Square, congratulated the capital city, which he said, ". . . had opened the innings for England with 150 not out."

Wings for Victory Award, 1943.
(Photograph courtesy Kidwelly Town Council).

"In Wales," he continued, "special mention must be made of Kidwelly in Carmarthenshire, who challenged London to reach its target first, and won. Kidwelly has now passed the £50,000 mark, their original target being £15,000."

1949 – 600 Jobs
The new factory under construction near the Tinplate Works was almost completed. The structure had been acquired by the British American Optical Co. Ltd., who would be employing 600 people.

1956 April – New Fire Station
Kidwelly firemen were praised by M.P. Sir Rhys Hopkin Morris, QC when he opened Kidwelly's new Fire Station. The depot was desperately needed as the old one was very much the worse for wear, was insubstantial and a disgrace to the town. Among the many guests who attended the opening ceremony were Ald. D. Hefin Evans, Mayor, Mr Ernald Jones, Town Clerk and J. E. Vaughan Evans, Town Surveyor.

1970s – President's Cup
Kidwelly RFC could claim many triumphs but their 'glory years' were without doubt in the 1970s when they dominated West Wales rugby. On three occasions in 1969/70, 1975/76 and 1979/80, they lifted the President's Cup. This most highly prized trophy in WWRU circles is achieved in a match played between the winners of the championship and winners of cup competitions. Responsible skippers to scoop this prestigious cup were – Marlston Morgan, Alan Williams and John Chapman.

1970s – League and Cup Double
In the 1970s Kidwelly Cricket Club dominated the Carmarthenshire League under the leadership of Gwyndaf Jones, captain of the team. The squad were league champions on six occasions and were winners of the challenge cup four times. The squad were successful in winning the League and Cup Double on four occasions – in 1974, 77, 78, 79.

1971 – 9-3
A famous scoreline, Llanelli 9, New Zealand 3. Mynydd-y-Garreg's Ray Gravell was chosen to play centre in the superb Scarlets team that unforgettably beat the All Blacks in a highly acclaimed match.

Great excitement prevailed throughout the district at that time and everyone knew and chanted the following snappy witticism –

> Who beat the All Blacks
> Who beat the All Blacks
> Who beat the All Blacks
> But good old Sospan Fach

Ray went on in his chosen career to win several caps with the Wales Rugby team.

Claim to Fame

Derek Clarke of Station Road in Kidwelly, member of the splendid Scarlets team, was chosen to play prop forward against the All Blacks in 1953 and Hywel Jones of Ferry Road, member of the elite Scarlets team, was selected to play second row forward against the All Blacks in 1963.

It is perhaps noteworthy to record that to my knowledge in Kidwelly these three rugby players only have been honoured to play first-class Rugby against the renowned All Blacks squad.

1978 – Champions

Kidwelly Town Bowling Club won the Llanelli & District Bowling League Championship on two occasions, in 1978 and 1981, under the captaincy of Wynne John and Phil Jones.

1988 – Double Champions

Kidwelly Town AFC's most successful season came to fruition in 1988/89 with both first and second teams winning their divisions. The senior side lifted the Carmarthenshire League Division 2 trophy under the leadership of skipper Mike Griffiths and the second team won the Reserve Championship under the direction of skipper Malcolm Morris.

May 2001 – Canolfan Tywysoges Gwenllian (Princess Gwenllian Centre)

Many, many years of talk and no action had at long last yielded results in the construction of a new hall in Station Road, located at the southern end of the town.

In August 1937 a carnival and sports event was held at Park Stephens. Chairman of the organising committee, John Jones of The Grove in Causway Street, promised that all proceeds would be used

*Just opened . . . Rhodri Morgan, First Secretary, attended the official opening
of the Canolfan Tywysoges Gwenllian. Also pictured is (from left to right),
Nesta Thomas, David Johns, Marie Higgins, ten-year-old Sophie Davies,
along with Rhodri Morgan and David Gravell.*
(Photograph courtesy *Llanelli Star*, 2001).

to boost an account set one side towards the financial cost of a new
Public Hall and Institute.

In May 1948 the Kidwelly Welfare Association Committee discussed
a project for the erection of a new public hall which was badly needed
in the town. "It is hoped that the public will support the planned
events and that the Borough Council will assist to swell the funds
that are needed," said Hon. Sec. Major Glyn James of Castle Farm.

Since those early days numerous discussions had taken place in
connection with the need for a new hall and finally in the new
Millennium all those hopes and dreams became reality. Full credit
to the Town Council, members of the Steering Committee and everyone who worked so hard and patiently and whose ambitions and
convictions had now been fulfilled by the construction of this modern
multi-purpose community hall. First Minister Rhodri Morgan, AM,
MP, officially opened the hall, which had been named Princess
Gwenllian Centre and unveiled a commemorative plaque, on Saturday,
May 5th, 2001. The brand new hall was funded by a grant from the
Wales Council for Voluntary Action (WCVA) as well as donations
and equipment from local businesses.

The First Minister said: "The Princess Gwenllian Centre is a symbol
of what can be achieved by a community when it unites behind a
project. Initiatives like this can enrich people's lives. They can

regenerate our towns and villages. The WCVA's grant scheme has helped to make this happen in communities across Wales. It is great to see so many members of the community involved in driving the project through and in securing the funding. Kidwelly has an important place in the history of Wales. Princess Gwenllian was a great Welsh heroine. The centre will be continuing this proud tradition into the 21st century."

June 2003 – Award
Gravells, the largest employer of the local workforce employing 60 staff, are in receipt of yet another award. They were pronounced 'Dealer of Excellence 2002' by Messrs Renault UK as being one of the top dealers in the United Kingdom.

DISASTERS

1403 – Three Week Siege
During the Glyndŵr Rebellion, forces led by Henry Donne, breached the town walls and caused extensive damage to the town, particularly to the Shire Hall. However, the castle withstood a three week siege.

Church Spire Damage
The church building had suffered a fair amount of disasters; the spire had been damaged by lightning on three occasions – in 1481, 1658 and 1884.

The earliest catastrophe recorded in the Church Register chillingly conveys the atmospheric event:

> "Upon the 29th day of October 1481, the steeple of Kidwelly fell down by lightning and a clap of thunder between one and two o'clock in the afternoon. From lightning and tempest, from battle and murder, and from sudden death, Good Lord, deliver us."

With regard to the disaster of 1658 the extent of the damage was recorded in the reports presented by the churchwardens some twenty years later, at which time, surprisingly, repairs were still left undone:

> "The churchwardens of the Parish of Kidwelly at the Archdeacon's visitation at Carmarthen on 2nd May, 1679, make the following presentiment – we present the Church of Kid-

welly to be quite destroyed and fallen down since the 24th day of June, Anno Domini 1658. We present the font, bell ropes and all other things belonging to the said Church to be out of repair. We present the Church coffer is out of repair."

John Griffiths, Jenkin Meyricke – Churchwardens.

19th January, 1839 – Hurricane

The effects of a terrifying hurricane were severe, not only through extensive damage to several houses but in particular to the ancient and venerable church, which was badly mutilated. A large part of the roof had been stripped and lay exposed to the elements. Several windows were badly damaged with one window especially (a very large one) having almost every pane shattered. Repairs would prove to be very costly but due to the huge efforts of the Vicar, the Rev. W. Herbert, there was no interruption to the church services.

1877 June – Storm Damage

In June 1877 one heavy downpour of rain followed by another went on for 24 hours. On the Sunday afternoon water gushed like a raging torrent down Ferry Road, into New Street and down to the town bridge. The water flooded into Capel Sul and all the houses in New Street, leaving a vast amount of damage in its wake. The storm played havoc on the roads as well, because when the waters subsided, torn up parts of the road were visible and heaps of stones had accumulated in other parts.

November 1883 – Serious Accident to Irish Express

Railway collisions are happily rare on this section of the Great Western Railway as there is a double line and block system in place. By this method no train leaves a station until the line is clear to the next, but despite all human precautions, accidents will happen. It was believed that long hours of service to which railway workers were subject, had much to answer for by way of accidents. Whether this one occurred for that reason was for the expected Board of Trade enquiry to decide.

There was terrific work pressure in Kidwelly Goods Department at the time, due mainly to the bustling activities of the tin, brick and lime industries in the area, all of which were interconnected by small branch lines.

One very wet Friday night, W. Lewis working alone on night shift and soaked to the skin, was being kept extremely busy as several goods trains needed to be sidetracked. At about 4.30 a.m. on the

Saturday morning, a down-goods train had been shunted into a crescent-shaped siding which ran alongside the up-line between the station and goods shed. The train was a very long one and some empty trucks overlapped onto the main line, because unfortunately the points were open. Also, Lewis could not see the end of the train from where he was working, which reinforced the situation already fraught with serious consequences.

The up-line Irish Express, comprising engine and tender, one tri-composite, one third-class, one composite coach, guards van, four horse boxes and two other vans, left Neyland at 2.45 a.m. and was due any minute. Believing the line to be clear, the points controller gave an 'all right' signal and the express travelling at high speed and gaining momentum at the Tanlan incline, crashed right through the rogue goods trucks. The collision was horrendous!! The goods wagons were so completely demolished, the exact number could only be ascertained by counting the wheels strewn around. The axle and pair of wheels became lodged under the front part of the engine, creating a brake-like action, slowing it down and checking its disruptive progress. It came to a halt a distance of about 150 yards away and tilted onto its right hand side.

One of the three trucks not destroyed in the crash was thrown one and a quarter miles up-line by the force of the impact, but apart from its frame and wheels the engine was free of any damage.

Miraculously, the driver and fireman escaped with no real injuries. They behaved like the true heroes they were, stood their ground and stayed at their posts, in all probability preventing further turmoil and destruction.

In the midst of all the chaos one elderly lady of Irish descent, to everyone's amusement, had lost a red petticoat and would not leave the coach without it.

There were about 48 other passengers, amazingly all unhurt.

Apparently unaware of why there was a hold-up, another passenger – an Irishman – stuck his head out a window and complained that there was no light.

The four horses at the rear end of the train did not fare so well, as three of the animals, said to be valued at £300, were badly injured. The groom on duty in one of the horseboxes at the time, was thrown clean out through a window coming down onto his feet with hardly a scratch.

There was no serious impairment to the tracks but damage to the rolling stock was estimated to be in the region of £5,000.

A huge breakdown gang arrived on the scene, followed by Inspector Miles of Carmarthen who was later joined by officials from Swansea to survey and evaluate the effects of the catastrophe. On appraising the scene, one inspector concluded it was the most serious accident he had ever come across in this part of the country. Both sets of tracks were blocked for quite some hours and a down-train and the up-train leaving Carmarthen at 5.45 p.m. could not get through. Repairs to the line took the best part of five hours but at 10 o'clock the down-line was clear and traffic resumed by using a single track.

The accident caused delays and blocks on the rail traffic, especially the Burry Port and Gwendraeth lines. Even so, on the Friday the Valley sent down 80 trucks as it was a busy time of the year for all the industries using the line.

To round off it is relevant to record that W. Lewis who was on duty at the time of the accident was said to be a steady and competent employee, and was also said to be very upset. However, it was claimed he was overworked and had asked for assistance while on night duty. It was considered that the blame lay with those who expected Lewis to do all the work without assistance.

Church Struck by Lightning 1884
On Friday morning shortly before 3 a.m. the inhabitants of Kidwelly were woken by a fearful tremor followed by a loud clattering which

Saint Mary's Church Steeple – storm damaged, February 1884.
(Photograph: Author).

Town Square, 1884. Note the extensive storm damage to the church steeple.
(Photograph courtesy Kidwelly Town Council).

St Mary's Church and the Castle, 2003.
(Photograph: Author).

went on for some time. The occupants of houses situated near to St Mary's Church said that right up to dawn, the sound of heavy pieces of masonry could be heard as they collapsed and plummeted to the ground. Daylight emerged and the townspeople were traumatised and frightened at the sight that met their eyes. The top part of the steeple had disappeared on one side leaving a gap of about 20-30 feet. The remaining part, which was bent like a bow with jagged irregular edges, looked as though it might topple over at any moment, threatening further turmoil to the chaos below. It was obvious that during the storm which raged throughout the night the tower had been struck on the southern side by a thunderbolt. The falling masonry, with impetus increased because of the height of the structure, crashed through the roof causing broken tiles and woodwork to add to the mountain of rubble already stockpiled on the ground. A closer examination revealed the state of the edifice was even worse than had appeared at first sight. The roof to the northern side had been completely destroyed, and huge boulders buried in the soft sward bore testimony to the force with which they had descended. Surveying the scene from amid the graves, the eyes beheld a building which seemed to have been overrun by a siege, nothing but debris everywhere and the dismantled tower exposed in all its nakedness.

The state of the houses in the vicinity could lend credence to this view. Holes yawned on many a roof and there was no scarcity of broken panes. On entering the church, evidence of overwhelming destruction was to be seen everywhere. One part of the church beneath the tower was open to the sky, with only a rafter here and a beam there to show that a roof had ever existed. The stones and masonry welded together by the cement, had been hurtled down with terrific force, against which, the wood seating had offered but frail resistance. Indents in the floor indicated that a stone had bounced from seat to seat, as if purposefully adding to the destruction of the visitation. A font, believed to be as ancient as the church itself, was smashed into unrecognisable fragments. The ball which was wont to rear itself so proudly on the eminence of the tower, was broken into two pieces. The pieces lay on the gallery floor, along with pieces of the coping and the parapet which had accompanied them during their descent. The clock components had been affected by the electricity, and the clock itself, as if to record the exact time of the incident, had stopped at 2.45. The weights were disarranged and one of the dials had sunk by about a foot. The wire which had joined with it was burnt, and a cask protecting the well through which they passed, was burnt to a cinder. The hoops were charred and dangled at the sides. Being unable to bear the strain wrought upon it, the sounding board above the peal of bells, had been driven down until the bells were hidden in the debris. There was some disquiet that the bells were cracked. The damaged side of the steeple remained in potential danger of falling to further annihilate the building.

November 1892 – Relief Fund
As there was no sign of a restart to production at the Gwendraeth Tin Plate Works, there was great distress in the area. The works had been shut down since May and most of the 700 employees were still out of work. Town Mayor Mr Daniel Stephens had set up a relief fund and dispensed with the conventional Mayor's Banquet in order to donate the function money to the fund.

March 1893 – Fatal Accident
A fatal accident occurred when a horse and trap returning from a funeral at Horeb Chapel bolted outside the Cawdor Arms, Bridge Street, Kidwelly. The horse and trap, owned by Evan Lewis of Panteg Farm, Llandefeilog, raced up Pinged Hill, down Pendre Hill and collided with a wall at Tycoch Bridge, bringing about a tragic fatality.

January 1896 – People Destitute
The full effect of the 'depression' took hold when the Kidwelly Tin Plate Works was closed and the men were paid off. The closure lasted for nearly four years and the consequences were calamitous. Some 150 families lived precariously on the verge of destitution, dependent largely on funds raised by public subscriptions. The Vicar, the Rev. D. Daven Jones, set up a soup kitchen in the Parish Room and provided about a quart of soup and a twopenny loaf of bread once a week.

December 1922 – Gas Works Flooded
Very heavy rain caused the ground on which the Gas Works was built to become so saturated that water leaked into the furnace pits. Great difficulty arose in trying to keep the fires going and re-vitalize the energy necessary to light the town properly. Consequently, in order to provide adequate domestic lighting, most of the street lamps were left unlit.

March 1926 – Soup Kitchen
Industries were badly penalised in this locality because of the first General Strike. Through the escalation of industrial action in the Llanelly area, many people became destitute and soup kitchens were organized in a number of districts, including Kidwelly. In the Gwendraeth Valley, over 7,000 miners were out on strike, many of whom were living in this area.

Miners Strike Soup Kitchen, 1926.
(Photograph: Author).

22nd June, 1957 – Aircraft Crash

An enquiry into the reason for the crash of a Hunter Aircraft on the main London-Fishguard railway line, about 200 yards from Kidwelly Station took place. Trainee pilot F. W. Jaques was killed in the accident and one of the points at issue was why had he not baled out sooner. It was believed that the ejection seat was not actuated until the aircraft was only 70 feet above the ground. Eye witness, Mrs M. Hubber of Tycoch Cottage, situated a distance of approximately 150 yards away from the railway line, said that the plane (which had taken off at the same time as another at Pembrey) appeared to be in trouble at the outset. She said she saw both planes heading towards Kidwelly; one climbed normally but the wings of the second plane dipped violently from side to side. She went on to say – "Finally, it dived onto the railway embankment and I heard three distinct explosions."

May 1965 – Factory Closure

Sixteen dejected men clocked out for the last time at the silent Royal Ordnance Factory at Pembrey, the day the factory was finally closed. Vigorous efforts to keep the factory open had gone on for several years. In the early part of 1962, when the rundown of the labour force was being considered, 1,052 workers were employed at the factory, a large proportion of that number being inhabitants of Kidwelly and district.

February 1972

One-third of the workforce employed at the British American Optical Co. Ltd., were to be made redundant because of the drop in demand for ophthalmic lenses. At the beginning of March, 230 employees would be dismissed and out of work. The factory, which at the time employed 709 people, would be re-organized to a single shift system.

3

Sport and Entertainment

SPORT

August 1886 – Football Club
Mayor Ald. D. Phillips, in the chair at a meeting of the Kidwelly Town Council recommended that unless the Parks Committee received one-third of all takings from the Football Club, the Committee be authorised to remove the goal posts from the park.

November 1903 – Horse Racing
The Kidwelly Steeplechase was held on November 2nd with runners Ancient Collier, King Cole and Saddler being some of the registered entries. The event, which had all the markings of an exciting occasion, took place at a racecourse in the Brickyard fields located near the Quay area.

January 1905 – Hockey Team
Kidwelly Hockey Team played a hard fought game at Ferryside which ended in a two-all draw. Kidwelly scorers were D. R. Wild and Saunders Davies.

1924 – Billiards
A very interesting billiards match between Ponthenry YMCA and the local Ex-servicemen's team took place at the British Legion Clubroom. The visitors ran out winners with T. H. Hussey and J. Conniff the pick of the home side.

July 1924 – Tennis
Kidwelly West End Tennis Team visited Carway hardcourts for a friendly. Afterwards, a sumptuous repast was provided in the pavilion, and on a motion passed by Capt. Cook (s.s. *Pelican*), seconded by Capt. Rocke, grateful thanks were extended to the ladies responsible.

December 1930 – Billiards/Snooker
On Christmas Eve, the final of the Billiards/Snooker Tournament was held at the Kidwelly Library and Institute. A large audience saw winners D. Williams of Station Road and D. J. Davies of Pinged Hill receive the prize of a turkey each. The birds were donated by Sir Alfred Stephens, JP, of Broomhill and John Thomas, JP, of Velindre House. D. Morlais Harry received a pair of fowl, as he was runner-up in both competitions.

1932 – Clay Pigeon Shooting
Mr Harry Jones of Paris House in Bridge Street, reputed to be a 'crack shot', was awarded a Silver Cup for winning at the Welsh Open Clay Pigeon Championship competition.

June 1937 – Quoits
Kidwelly's Gwendraeth Town Quoits team, skippered by Islwyn Evans, were away to Ferryside on Saturday. At the end of a 'good' game, Kidwelly returned home victorious by 18 shots.

December 1942 – Rugby Football
The RFC squad (including several Kidwelly exiles), defeated an RAF Pembrey team at a match on Christmas morning at Park Stephens. A large crowd had come together to watch the game which was well controlled by referee, Stan Maliphant.

February 1947 – Cricket
Kidwelly Cricket Club held a well attended Annual General Meeting at the Lord Nelson Inn. Club Chairman, Mr Sam Evans, thanked everyone who supported the club and reported a balance in hand of £62.3s.0d. Later on in the evening a presentation was made to Club Secretary Mr Llew Rees, a former team captain, in recognition of 20 years of faithful service to cricket in the town.

May 1954 – Bowls
A Bowls Club was formed during a meeting held in the Town Hall with Mayor, Ald. John Rees, in the chair. Mr T. W. Thomas was elected President, Mr N. L. Johnson Secretary and Mr Emlyn Jones was chosen to be Chairman and Club Captain.

Kidwelly RFC 1941-42.
Top row, left to right: *Idris Griffiths, Glan Griffiths, Sid Lewis, ?, Len Hoskins, Reg Anstee, Ron Johns, Gwyn Griffiths, Wyndham Thomas, Tom Lewis.*
Middle row: *Len Conniff, John Williams, Harry Manners (Chairman), Harold Rees (Captain), Vincent Griffiths, Alwyn Evans.*
Front row: *Alec Lewis, Arthur Lewis.*
(Photograph courtesy Kidwelly R.F.C.).

Kidwelly AFC 1959.
Standing, left to right: *Malcolm Evans, Clive Davies, Tony Thorburn, Ray Foligno, Derek Fisher, Edmund Gravell, Hubert Baker (Trainer).* Front row: *John Thomas, Wyn Hughes, Mansel Rees (Captain), Trevor Jones, Sefton Cresser.*
(Photograph courtesy Lord Nelson Inn).

1959 – Association Football
A soccer side was established in the town when Kidwelly Town AFC
was reformed and entered the Carmarthenshire League in 1959. The
committee included: Chairman Ken Barry (the Stationmaster), Aelwyn
Jones, Secretary, Hubert Baker, Trainer and Glyn Davies was elected
Club President. The team played on Brickyard field, making their
way to the pitch about a quarter of a mile away from their head-
quarters at the Castle Hotel.

March 1962 – Table Tennis
St Mary's Church Table Tennis Club accompanied by the Rev. David
G. Williams, travelled to Llansaint for a match with the church team
of All Saints. The home side, led by Ferryside curate Rev. P. L. Fenton,
were the winners on this occasion.

ENTERTAINMENT

October 1894 – St Luke's Fair
Despite the weather there was a large attendance at the St Luke's Fair
held on Monday and Tuesday. A shortage of both male and female
servants resulted in higher than usual rates of pay on offer. Cattle
sold well on the Monday and there was a brisk trade of pigs on
Tuesday. The familiar sideshows, shooting galleries, merry-go-rounds
and the many other entertainments also turned up as usual at this
ever popular business/pleasure two-day festival.

1914 – Eisteddfod
An Eisteddfod was held in the castle under the auspices of St Mary's
Welsh Sunday School. A large turn-out, favourable weather and first-
class performances made for an excellent day.

December 1916 – Charlie Chaplin
The Charlie Chaplin competition at Kidwelly Cinema proved to be
a great success. Ivor Rees of Pontnewydd won first prize, second prize
was won by Harry Gower and consolation prizes were awarded to
Arthur Hughes and D. J. King.

Late 1920s – 'Y Parti Bach'
The Kidwelly Male Voice Glee Party came about when a number of
men who were gathered together on the grain (a mound outside the

entrance to the castle) began singing. "Why not form a male voice choir?" was suggested, and they did, as recalled by Mr Gwyn Rees. Mr John Islwyn Evans was appointed conductor and Mr David John Rees became their accompanist. The choir was nicknamed 'Y Parti Bach' because there was only a small number of voices in the group. The choir practised at Capel Sul Chapel and at the Town Hall. Later, they enrolled new members, expanded the choir and became known as 'The Castellwyr Male Voice Party'. They went on to achieve great success, winning numerous first prizes in competitions, as can be seen by the number of trophies displayed in the photograph.

May 1921 – Quartet Prize
At the Eisteddfod held at Pembrey, first prize in the Quartet Section with 'Brightly dawns our Wedding Day' was awarded to Mr W. J. Rees, Kidwelly, and friends.

June 1922 – Chaired Bard
An Eisteddfod was held at the castle on Whit Monday and proved a great success. Large crowds of people arrived by rail, motor cars and pony and trap. One of the adjudicators was the Rev. D. Ambrose Jones, BA, Vicar of Kidwelly. Among the local successes were Mr David D. T. Rees of Kidwelly who won the tenor solo. The chaired bard was the Rev. E. J. Herbert, Minister at Morfa Chapel. Success of the day was attributed to hard-working secretary, Cllr. E. J. Gower, and a hard-working committee.

January 1923 – Tennis Club Dance
A very successful dance and whist drive organised by the Tennis Club took place at the Town Hall. Prizes were donated by Mr J. Rocke of the Bakery and Club Chairman Mr A. P. Mansel. The large crowd at the event enjoyed the evening where MCs Idris Jones and Melville White served at the whist drive, and MC Tom Lewis served at the dance.

November 1926 – November Fair
Mrs Elizabeth Walton of the Pelican Inn in Bridge Street applied for a special licence for concessions during the November Fair. There was no objection and a licence was granted.

December 1930 – Masked Dance
Kidwelly RFC held their annual masked dance on Christmas Eve at the Town Hall. Joint MCs were Gwilym Hughes of Gwendraeth Town

Y Castellaur Male Glee Party, 1933.
Back row, left to right: *Thomas John Hughes, WIlliam Jones, WIlliam Morgan, David Davies, Eddie Powell, Richard Evans, Gwyn Morris, Jack Richards.* Third row: *Llewelyn Williams, Walter Cole, David Phillips, John Wild, Bertie Davies, Samuel Evans, Harry Gower, Stanley Rees.* Second row: *William Evans, David Harries, Harry Bunyan, David Johns, T. J. Bevan, Melville White, Robert John, Charles Gibbard, Glan Evans, Gwyn Rees.* Front row: *Gomer Morris, David Thorburn, WIllliam J. Rees, David John Rees (Accompanist), John Islwyn Evans (Conductor), Edward Richards, David Davies, Tom Evans, Simon Gravell.*
(Photograph courtesy Moira and Mali Richards).

and Frank John, Felindre. Music was provided by Henry John Owens and the new Windsor Band.

December 1934 – Christmas Chocolate and Orange
Mrs Foy, co-manager of Kidwelly Cinema and her assistant Miss Hilda Evans, handed out a bar of chocolate and an orange to each child attending a Saturday matinee, a special gift to celebrate the Christmas Festival.

1942 – Solo Winner
Mr George Thomas of Ferry Road won the Baritone Solo Competition at the National Eisteddfod of Wales held in Cardigan.

1946 – The Pilgrim's Chorus
The Castellwyr Male Voice Choir won first prize in the first competition they entered which took place at Bronwydd near Carmarthen. They were conducted by Mr John Islwyn Evans with Miss Mair Rowlands being accompanist. Numerous first prizes were awarded to them for their rendering of Dr Joseph Parry's 'The Pilgrim's Chorus' with George Thomas being the soloist. The choir travelled all over Wales, entered 30 competitions in just over twelve months, yet still finding time to hold concerts at various locations.

They won the shield at Aberystwyth twice, in 1948 and 1950, and travelled as far afield as North Wales, Lampeter and Glynneath to compete. Unlike many other choirs of that era they were not afraid to enter contests at Morriston, where the famous Morriston Orpheus Choir frightened many competitors away.

In 1951 and 1952 the choir competed at the International Eisteddfod at Llangollen where they put up credible performances against international competition.

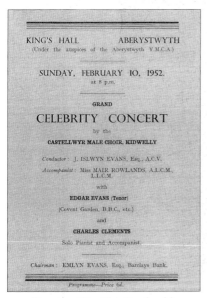

(Courtesy Miss Mair Rowlands).

October 1947 – London Show
David Griffiths (known locally as Dewi Griffiths) of Ferry Road, a
well-known vocalist with a regular broadcasting slot on radio,
appeared in the show 'Annie Get your Gun' at London's Colosseum
Theatre.

November 1947 – Variety Bandbox
Mr John Jones (known locally as John Amos), son of Cllr. J. Amos
Jones of Ferry Road, appeared with celebrity Frankie Howerd on
Variety Bandbox, the popular radio programme.

July 1948 – Carnival
Kidwelly Carnival attracted a large crowd to Park Stephens. Winners
who were awarded prizes were – Original Adult, Mrs Hubber of
Tycoch; Comic Adult, Mrs Mu Lane of Priory Street, and best dressed
couple were Roy Williams and Roy Lloyd.

1956 – Mixed Choir
A Kidwelly and District mixed choir was formed mainly of church
and chapel members. Mr Terry James conducted the choir and Miss

KIDWELLY EISTEDDFOD CHOIR	ARTISTES.
present	JOAN ROWLANDS-REES .... Soprano.
E L I J A H	SAL THOMAS .... Contralto.
(Mendelssohn)	ERYL COSLETT .... Tenor.
	GEORGE THOMAS ... . Bass.
at	ROSEMARY HUBBER.. .... Youth.
CAPEL SUL	MARY BUNYAN, ROSEMARY HUBBER and MARGARET THOMAS .. Trio,
on	THE PHILLIP EDWARDS ORCHESTRA
WEDNESDAY and THURSDAY, 26th and 27th September, 1956	(Leader : PHILLIP EDWARDS)
at 7.00 p.m.	Accompanist ' : MAIR ROWLANDS
	Conductor : TERRY JAMES
in aid of	
THE EISTEDDFOD FUND	CHAIRMAN (Wednesday) : HIS WORSHIP,THE MAYOR of KIDWELLY, (Counc. D.J. LLOYD, J.P.)
	CHAIRMAN (Thursday) : THE CHAIRMAN, CARMARTHENSHIRE COUNTY COUNCIL, (C.C. J. AMOS JONES)
Programme .... 3d.	

(Courtesy Miss Mair Rowlands).

'Elijah' Concert 1956.

Left to right: *Phillip Edwards (Leader of Orchestra), Sal Thomas (Contralto), Terry James (Conductor), Cllr. D. J. Lloyd (Mayor of Kidwelly, Chairman), Joan Rowlands-Rees (Soprano), George Thomas (Bass), Mair Rowlands (Accompanist).*
(Photograph courtesy Miss Mair Rowlands).

Mair Rowlands was the accompanist. Singing at Capel Sul to packed houses they astonishingly performed 'Elijah', 'The Messiah', 'Creation' and 'Hymn of Praise', all in a time span of just over twelve months.

August 1956 – Air Display
A well attended Air Show was arranged by RAF Pembrey. Children were fascinated and delighted with the display which took place in the skies over the town of Kidwelly. Highlight of the event was a display of four Hawker Hunters flying in tight formation giving a thrilling and excellent performance. The famous Canberra and the newly-announced Javelin also made their appearance to the wonderment of everyone present.

March 1959 – Albert Hall
Mr Terry James, well-known and prestigious musician, conducted a performance of famous musical pieces and hymns by massed choirs of Wales at the Albert Hall to celebrate St David's Day.

December 1965 – Silver Band Waggon
Mynydd-y-Garreg Silver Band members drove around the town and played Christmas carols in a lorry fitted up for the occasion with seats, lighting and a large plastic sheet for protection in the inclement weather. Under the conductorship of Mr D. T. Gravell, 2 night/4 hour tours took place in the village, at Four Roads and at Kidwelly.

October 1969 – 'Bore Da'
Mrs Danny Mitchell of 1 Ger-y-Castell, a member of Kidwelly Women's Institute, gave a most enlightening talk on the BBC Radio programme 'Bore Da' (Good Morning).

December 1972 – Christmas Carols
Kidwelly Town Band, led by Mr Eddie Charlton, played Christmas Carols around the town in order to raise funds towards the upkeep of equipment. They collected a total of £55.

1983 – Festival Choir
The Kidwelly Festival Choir was inaugurated following the Year of the Castles in 1983 – hence the name Côr Gŵyl Cydweli. The actual formation took place in January 1984 at a public meeting in the old Community Centre, when Mr Tal John was appointed its first chair-

man and Mrs Catherine Francis its conductor for the first year. Thereafter, Mrs Francis became the permanent conductor until 1996. The inspiration to form a mixed choir in Kidwelly was due to Dr Terry James who at the time was pursuing a distinguished musical career in the USA.

The first Annual Concert was held in St Mary's Church, Kidwelly, in November 1984. St Mary's remained the venue for all subsequent annual concerts. The choir was supportive of numerous charitable causes.

The choir also performed with Côr Meibion Dowlais at the 1994 St David's Festival at the Rhydycar Leisure Centre, Merthyr Tydfil, at St John Lloyd's School, Llanelli, in 1993, at the Newquay Cornwall Festival in 1995, and two visits to the 'Thousand Voices' at the Albert Hall in 1987 and 1993.

A Choral Exchange was formed with a choir from Nieder, Liebersbach, Germany, in 1995. The German choir visited Kidwelly in 1986 and 1990 and The Kidwelly choir visited Germany in 1988 and 1993, with several concerts performed in both countries.

4

Arsenic Poisoning Trial

THE GREENWOOD TRIAL 1920

Mystery is still Unsolved

Arsenic Trial Makes History

A trait of human nature is curiosity about crime, especially the violent sort. It grips the imagination of society as a whole, and infamous crimes and trials have succeeded in captivating large masses of the populace. Over 80 years ago a trial in Carmarthen was given world-wide coverage which caught the attention of the British public.

The circumstances surrounding the Greenwood trial which took place in 1920 caused a sensation, when Harold Greenwood was tried for the murder of his wife, Mabel, mother of his four children, and even today is quite often talked about in the locality.

Was he guilty? Did the brilliant skill of one barrister turn the case?

DIARY OF EVENTS

1919

June 16th	Death of Mrs Mabel Greenwood; cause certified to be 'heart disease'.
June 19th	Mrs Greenwood buried in St Mary's churchyard.
October 1st	The widower marries Miss Gladys Jones, daughter of a Llanelly newspaper proprietor.
October 24th	Greenwood interviewed by police because of rumours in the village.

1920

April 16th	Body of Mrs Greenwood exhumed.
June 8th	Scotland Yard inquiries begin.

June 16th	Coroner's Jury certifies she died from arsenic, administered by her husband. Harold Greenwood arrested and taken to Llanelly jail.
July 3rd	Greenwood was committed to the next Carmarthen Assizes to stand trial on the charge of murder.
November 2nd	The trial commences at Carmarthen Guildhall.
November 8th	The jury returned a verdict, 'Not Guilty'.

PERSONS INVOLVED IN THE DRAMA

Mr Harold Greenwood, solicitor, 46.
Mrs Mabel Greenwood, deceased, 47.
Miss Irene Greenwood, daughter.
Mr Kenneth Greenwood, son.
Miss Edith Bowater, sister of the deceased.
Miss Gladys Amelia Jones, clerk, the second Mrs Greenwood.
Mr William Jones, proprietor of the *Llanelly Mercury* newspaper and
    father of Gladys Jones.

Harold Greenwood
. . . *'weakness for the ladies'.*
(Photograph courtesy Dr Terry James).

Mabel Greenwood
. . . *'arsenic found in body'.*
(Photograph courtesy Dr Terry James).

Dr Thomas R. Griffiths, family doctor.

Miss Mary Griffiths, sister of the doctor.

Miss Elizabeth Louise Jones, district nurse.

Miss Florence Lorraine Phillips, close friend of the first Mrs Greenwood.

Miss Hannah Maggie Williams, parlour-maid, Rumsey House.

Mrs Martha Morris, servant, Rumsey House.

Miss Margaret Ann Morris, cook, Rumsey House.

Miss Lily Gwyneira Powell, between stairs maid, Rumsey House.

Mr William Gold, gardener, Rumsey House.

Mr Benjamin Williams, handyman, Rumsey House.

Mrs Grove, caretaker at Harold Greenwood's Llanelly office.

Mrs Smart, local nurse.

Rev. D. Ambrose Jones, vicar of the Parish.

Mr Thomas Foy, chauffeur and local cinema proprietor.

Miss Mary Morris, telephone operator Kidwelly Exchange.

Mr Clifford Jones, chemist, Bridge Street, Kidwelly.

William & Sarah Edwards, proprietors Phoenix Wine Store, Bridge Street, Kidwelly.

Supt. Samuel Jones, Llanelly Police, in charge of the case.

Sgt. Hodge Lewis, Kidwelly Police.

Insp. Nicholas, Llanelly Police.

Chief Insp. Ernest Haigh of Scotland Yard.

Mr Justice Shearman, Presiding Judge.

Sir Edward Marlay Samson, KC for the prosecution.

Sir Edward Marshall Hall, KC for the defence.

Dr John Webster, Government Analyst.

Dr William Henry Wilcox, Home Office Pathologist.

Few of the thousands who regularly pass the imposing walls of a certain Kidwelly chapel located in the main thoroughfare, Bridge Street, overlooking the Gwendraeth Fach River, know of the macabre mystery that surrounded the Georgian-style building more than 80 years ago. The chapel, now known as Capel Sul, was at that time home of a Llanelly solicitor, Mr Harold Greenwood, and the building was called Rumsey House. Built in 1862 by T. W. A. Evans the name reflected Rumsey House, Caine, Wilts., his mother's family home.

The Greenwoods married in 1896 and *The Times* newspaper recorded the following notice in the Marriages column – "Harold Greenwood, youngest son of Norman William Greenwood Esq., of

Rumsey House, Kidwelly.
(Photograph courtesy Brynmor Evans).

Greenwood Lean, Inglewood, Yorkshire and Mabel Bowater, daughter of William Vansittart Bowater, Baronet, Bury Hall, Edmonton, Middx.". In 1898 they moved to Kidwelly, first to Broomhill, then later on to The Priory, Lady Street. The same year Harold Greenwood was taken on as a solicitor by a firm in Llanelly. Later on he started his own practice in an office in Frederick Street, Llanelly.

The Greenwoods moved into Rumsey House in November 1916. Both were well-known in the town; Mabel Greenwood was popular, took an interest in town affairs, and was a very devoted woman who regularly attended St Mary's Church. She also attended all the charities and fêtes and supported the local tennis and croquet clubs.

Greenwood on the other hand does not seem to have been very popular. He was legal adviser to money lenders in a town where there was financial hardship, and an acquaintance at that time described him as 'not having a single man friend'. However, he was popular with the ladies, he had a roving eye, and gossips at times accused him of 'carrying on'. His most interesting 'acquaintanceship' was with Miss Mary Griffiths, sister to Dr Griffiths.

Mrs Greenwood was a woman of not very good health. She was 47 years of age, had borne four children – Irene, Kenneth, Eileen and Ivor; she had a weak heart and suffered fainting attacks. Her doctor for over 17 years was Dr Thomas Griffiths, who had a sister Mary, 30 years of age, who helped her bachelor brother with house

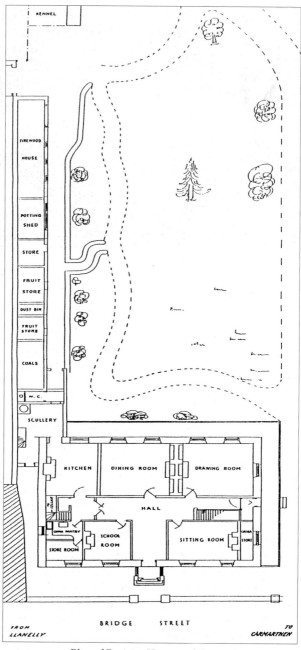

Plan of Rumsey House and Grounds.

Kidwelly Cricket Club, 1907.
Back row, left to right: *T. Thomas, Irving Davies, W. Walters (Vice-Captain),*
R. Davies, W. Dun Davies, W. Thomas (Secretary).
Middle row: *James Watkins, G. E. Bowen, J. H. Elias (Captain),*
Harold Greenwood, Harry Gravel, Dr T. R. Griffiths.
Front row: *Cliff Bowen, W. G. Lewis, D. J. Lewis.*

N.B.: *The photograph includes Harold Greenwood and Dr Tommy Griffiths,*
the first being the accused and the other being one of the chief
witnesses in the Arsenic Poisoning Trial in 1920.
(Photograph courtesy William Beynon).

surgery. A few months before Mrs Greenwood's death, the doctor suspected an internal growth in her abdominal region, but this was later found to be a non-malignant tumour.

In the early part of the last century, Kidwelly was a bustling little town. The tin works was in full operation, there were several functional silica brick works, there was a sawmill and the quarry. Harold Greenwood would have passed the main Stephens brick works daily as he commuted to his office in Llanelly by train. Greenwood's business brought him into contact with Mr William Jones, owner of a local newspaper (*Llanelly Mercury*), and his young daughter, Gladys. Over the years they became very good friends. He returned each evening to his wife and four children at Rumsey House, their well run home with a cook, parlour-maid, between stairs maid, daily cleaning woman and a gardener.

Mr Neville Jones, Pantycrug, recalls how his mother Mrs Marion

Jones, daughter of J. G. Anthony, Paris House General Stores, remembered Harold Greenwood coming into the shop regularly. She formed the opinion that he was a 'ladies man'. Paris House in Bridge Street was situated opposite Rumsey House, and as a young woman, Mrs Jones recalled serving Harold Greenwood in the shop, where he purchased tins of Cherry Blossom black boot polish. He was very insistent that the brand had to be Cherry Blossom – no other boot polish would do. She said he was a dapper little man, who always wore spats and his shoes were always gleaming with a mirror-like finish. When you consider we are talking about the 1920s, when roads and pavements were very dusty with few cars around, and mainly horse-drawn transport, Greenwood's shoes must have stood out like beacons.

Rumours arose concerning Mrs Greenwood's health because on Thursday, June 12th, 1919 (a few days prior to her death), Mr Greenwood had said his wife was looking ill. However, on Saturday, June 14th, she was seen to be very active, although one of her servants – Martha Morris – thought she looked ill that morning. Mrs Greenwood visited the Pheonix Wine Stores in Bridge Street and bought a bottle of burgundy from Mr William Edwards, the proprietor. There was subsequently contradictory evidence at the trial relating to the bottle of burgundy.

Despite all the talk about Mabel Greenwood's ill health she felt well enough in the Spring of 1919 to plan a holiday with her sister Miss Edith Bowater.

After lunch on the Saturday of June 14th, Mrs Greenwood accompanied by the vicar, the Rev. D. Ambrose Jones, caught a train to Ferryside to attend a tennis meeting. Tragically, this was the last time she would leave the house alive.

Harold Greenwood claimed he had warned his wife that the journey would be too fatiguing. Greenwood himself stayed at home all day. After tea, he called at the local telephone exchange and asked Miss Mary Morris the

Rev. D. Ambrose Jones.

telephone operator for the *Llanelly Mercury*. Who did he phone that day? The prosecution claimed it proved a close association with his second wife who was employed at the *Mercury* offices. Later in the evening Mrs Greenwood caught a train from Ferryside back to Kidwelly and walked home with her daughter Irene, who said that her mother seemed perfectly well, and nothing in any way unusual occurred that evening. Mrs Greenwood, although not enjoying the best health at times, believed in living life to the full. She retired to her bed at 10.15 p.m. – she and Harold slept in separate bedrooms.

Turning to the fateful day – Sunday, June 15th, the family had breakfast at 10.00 a.m. Greenwood said his wife sat in the garden, reading for most of the morning.

At 12.30 p.m. Hannah Williams, the parlour-maid, swore that Mr Greenwood went into the china pantry and remained there for half an hour. Greenwood himself said that he constantly used the sink in the china pantry to wash his hands having worked on the car, but sinister motives for that visit were to be described at the trial. He was repairing the car that morning with the assistance of Mr Tom Foy (who ran the local cinema). Giving evidence at the trial, Foy said he had been in Greenwood's company all morning.

Lunch was served at 1 p.m. with leg of lamb, roast beef and vegetables on the menu, followed by gooseberry tart and custard. At the trial, Hannah Williams swore that Greenwood drank whiskey, his wife drank burgundy and the children Irene and Kenneth drank water. The other children, Eileen and Ivor, were away at college. Mabel Greenwood drank some of the burgundy she had bought at the Phoenix Stores next door the previous day. Described on its red label as 'real pure wine', the prosecution stated at the trial it was anything but.

Gooseberry tart was served for pudding that day and Harold pointed out, "Mabel dear, do you not think that gooseberry tart is wise with your stomach condition."

"Nonsense," she replied, "they're from the garden."

A lunchtime visitor was Miss Florence Phillips, Y Bwthyn. In Kidwelly she was nicknamed 'the Kidwelly postman' because she was a well-known gossip. She was a close friend of Mrs Greenwood. After lunch, Irene had a driving lesson in her father's new car, her instructor was Tom Foy. Mabel Greenwood sat in the garden and had tea brought out to her. She showed signs of illness in the afternoon and at 3.30 p.m. said Greenwood, she suffered a severe attack of diarrhoea. Incidentally, this is a

Mr Tom Foy, gave lessons in motor driving to Miss Greenwood.

prominent symptom of arsenic poisoning. The Crown later sought to establish this was the first indication of Mrs Greenwood's fatal illness, occurring at the earliest time possible after lunch. Several witnesses, however, stated that Mrs Greenwood was well as late as 6 o'clock.

At 4.30 p.m. maid Hannah Williams brought out tea and said her mistress seemed normal at that time. Later on, at 6.30 p.m. during an after tea stroll, Mabel collapsed in the garden, complaining of sickness and suffering pain around the heart region. Harold gave his wife brandy, which she brought up instantly. Irene said, "Shall I fetch Dr Griffiths?"

"No, Irene," said Greenwood, "help me get her upstairs," and they struggled to get Mrs Greenwood up the stairs.

In the end, at 7 p.m., Dr Griffiths was called; he found his patient on a couch and vomiting. She told him the gooseberry tart had upset her, "as it always did." The doctor ordered her to take sips of brandy and soda water and she was taken to bed. Then, amazingly, the two men (doctor and husband) left Irene with her mother and played clock golf in the garden. Irene reported later that her mother was now suffering from diarrhoea as well. The doctor saw Mrs Greenwood before leaving for home and sent over a bottle of bismuth mixture dispensed by him personally.

Miss Phillips.

Miss Florence Phillips paid a return visit to see her close friend and found the place in uproar. On seeing Mrs Greenwood's condition she rushed out immediately to fetch the district nurse. On arrival, Nurse Jones found the ailing Mrs Greenwood cold and collapsed and she administered another dose of the medicine sent over by the doctor. "It seemed to me," the nurse stated later, "an ordinary bismuth mixture. I stayed with the patient from 8 to 9 o'clock; she was very weak but there was no change. I therefore decided to slip home to put my child to bed." Irene and Miss Phillips were left in charge.

Nurse Jones returned at 10 p.m. to find no change in the patient's condition. She gave her patient, who was by now very weak, brandy, milk, soda water and more brandy at 15 minute intervals, but all was vomited every time. In addition, the poor soul had diarrhoea of a sort the nurse had never in all her professional experience seen before.

The servants had been sent to bed and Miss Phillips was persuaded to go home at 11 o'clock. Harold Greenwood saw Miss Phillips off the premises and as she left Greenwood told her that: ". . . he had known his wife much worse and she would be all right in the morning." At the gate he saw Dr Griffiths taking his evening stroll. "How is your wife?" asked the doctor. "She is comfortable at present," replied Greenwood.

District Nurse Jones.

Nurse Jones reported a conversation she had with Mrs Greenwood who had said: "If anything happens to me I want my sister to bring up the children."

Mrs Greenwood's condition was deteriorating and the doctor was sent for again. During the night Dr Griffiths paid four visits to his patient. His evidence and that of Mr Greenwood, Miss Phillips and Nurse Jones varied somewhat as to exact times. Throughout the whole episode the doctor treated Mrs Greenwood for gastric trouble.

Another discrepancy in the evidence arose over Mr Greenwood calling the doctor at midnight. The prosecution alleged that Greenwood took over an hour to fetch the doctor, but Greenwood swore – and was backed up by Miss Mary Griffiths – that he took no more than 10 minutes.

Dr Griffiths was called by Greenwood again later on when Mrs Greenwood's condition deteriorated further. He returned, saying: "I could not rouse him." However, when Nurse Jones called at the doctor's house she roused him without any delay. The diarrhoea endured by Mrs Greenwood continued incessantly, but despite her suffering and discomfort, she was thoughtful and unselfish to a degree. She repeatedly apologised to the nurse for giving her trouble.

During the trial the type of pills prescribed by Dr Griffiths was hotly debated. The doctor said he gave them after the 10 p.m. visit, but the nurse and Greenwood said he gave them at 1 a.m. Mrs Greenwood collapsed into a coma or sleep after taking these pills and Greenwood said later the pills were too strong. Were the 'morphia pills', as Greenwood called them, the cause of death?

Mrs Greenwood died at 3.30 a.m. on Monday, 16th June, 1919. Her illness exhibited two known symptoms of arsenic poisoning –

vomiting and diarrhoea. Two other symptoms, namely cramp and thirst, were not evident.

Was it a case of poisoning by arsenic or were the pills prescribed by the doctor too strong? What were those pills? If they contained morphia, (everyone was of the opinion they were), they formed a lethal dose for a frail woman weakened by several hours of stomach purging. At the Police Inquest, Dr Griffiths said he had given the patient 'morphia pills' to ease her pain. At the trial he said he made a mistake at the inquest, and actually had prescribed 'opium pills'. Opium of course is only 10 per cent as strong as morphia.

The death certificate signed by Dr Thomas R. Griffiths stated that death was due to valvular disease of the heart.

The sudden death of a popular resident of Kidwelly shocked the townsfolk. Local papers politely mentioned her death in the obituary pages but this was only a beginning of the mysterious story surrounding Mabel Greenwood's untimely death.

Nurse Jones called at Kidwelly Vicarage on the morning following Mrs Greenwood's death and the vicar stated she was very much vexed over the whole affair.

As written in the book entitled *The Trial of Harold Greenwood*: "The earliest hint of a dreadful suspicion, which was ultimately to lead to a criminal charge, seems to have dated to this conversation between the local clergyman and the district nurse." The Rev. Ambrose Jones is said to have enquired whether there had been foul play in connection with Mrs Greenwood's death. Harold Greenwood's actions on the morning of his wife's death, did nothing to enhance his reputation. At 10 a.m. he called at the *Llanelly Mercury* office and he borrowed £20 from Gladys Jones, daughter of the proprietor. Later on in the day, he and the vicar chose a site for his wife's grave in Kidwelly churchyard.

On Thursday, 19th June, the vicar had to shout to make himself heard at the funeral service, due to the noise emanating from the vast number of people filling the church. Harold Greenwood arrived at the last minute, and again the vicar's suspicion was aroused by Greenwood's failure to bring the death certificate, even though it was perfectly in order. He had not even registered his poor wife's death; he had sent Irene to perform this task while he visited shops in search of mourning clothes.

While the Rev. Ambrose Jones had his suspicions, District Nurse Jones too was dubious about the events. At the funeral she met another local nurse – Mrs Smart, President of the Local Nursing Association.

Nurse Jones told her: "It was very sad for Mrs Greenwood to die so young, this case has worried me a lot. I have never seen anything like it before in my thirty years of nursing. I wish I had my time over again, I'd insist on a post-mortem, although I don't like them." Mrs Smart asked: "You don't think something was wrong?" "No," was the reply, "I don't think that, it's just that I'm not sure."

Nurse Jones visited Rumsey House on several occasions after the death of Mrs Greenwood but when she was later interviewed by the police, she said there was nothing unusual about the death.

Following the death of her sister, Miss Edith Bowater came to Rumsey House as Mistress of the House and had charge of the children as Mabel had expressly hoped during her last hours. She made no secret of her dislike of Harold Greenwood.

Harold Greenwood was aware of a certain coolness everywhere; his practice commitments (never that successful) dropped to almost zero. He appeared to be lonely – not so – in fact he was busy writing letters. May Griffiths, the doctor's sister, received a letter on 26th September, 1919 – three months after Mrs Greenwood's funeral. (May was the affectionate name Greenwood used to address Mary). This letter complicated their mysterious relationship somewhat. The letter read:

Rumsey House, Kidwelly
Carmarthenshire
(Friday)

Recipient of a much-discussed letter from Mr Greenwood, Miss Mary Griffiths.

Mr dearest May,

I have been trying hard to get to you this last fortnight, but no luck, always someone going in, or you were out. Now I want you to read this letter very carefully, and to think very carefully, and to send me over a reply tonight. There are very many rumours about, but between you and I this letter reveals the true position. Well, it is only right that you should know that Miss Bowater and Miss Phillips between them, have turned my children against you, very bitterly – why, I don't know. It is only right that you should know this, as you are the one I love most in the world, and I would be the last one to make you unhappy. Under these circumstances, are you prepared to face the music?

I am going to do something quickly, as I must get rid of Miss
Bowater at once, as I am simply fed up.

Yours as ever,
Harold

What was meant by the contents of this letter? What was Greenwood thinking when he wrote it? He was already engaged to Gladys
Jones of Llanelly and had given her an expensive ring.

There was a bad atmosphere in Rumsey House following Mabel
Greenwood's death. Miss Bowater, the new mistress of the house, did
not get on with Greenwood, and perhaps a marriage would be
Greenwood's way of getting rid of her.

Gossips in the town referred to something 'fishy' about Mabel
Greenwood's sudden death. The rumours accelerated when on July
12th Greenwood became engaged to Gladys Jones, the young Llanelly
woman, barely a month after his wife's death. Talk of a marriage
fanned even more the fires of suspicion.

Mrs Greenwood, second wife
of the Welsh solicitor.

On October 1st, 1919, Harold Greenwood and Gladys Jones were married
in Bryn Chapel, Llanelly, a mere 15
weeks after the funeral of his late wife.
Irene Greenwood had knowledge of
the marriage plan only two days ahead
of the ceremony. She was greatly
shocked and upset and left home to
live with relatives in London. The
second Mrs Greenwood was a woman
aged 30 and Harold had known her
since childhood. A friendship bond
between Greenwood and Gladys
Jones's family went back to 1898 when
Greenwood had assisted Mr William
Jones in his business. In consequence,
Gladys and the other children also
became friends of the family.

Kidwelly town, already rife with rumour and gossip, was shaken
to the core by this news of the philandering solicitor. There had been
successive comments and aspersions on Greenwood's friendship with
various women, his most interesting acquaintanceship being with
Mary Griffiths, sister of the doctor, which brings us back to the letter

he wrote her just a week before his marriage. Miss Griffiths insisted the letter was written in jest. At his trial, Greenwood admitted the letter was written by him, ". . . but at Miss Griffiths's request," he said. He also said that when he told her of his intended marriage to Gladys Jones she burst into tears, claimed he had let her down and demanded a letter from him to show she had been jilted. In the witness box Miss Griffiths denied practically all of Greenwood's account of the letter.

Shortly after Irene's departure, Miss Bowater also flounced out, deposed by the new mistress. What an awful homecoming it must have been for Gladys and Harold – an empty house, neighbours crossing the road to avoid them and the whole town buzzing with rumour.

Greenwood's marriage gave a fresh impetus to the sinister 'whispers' flying around in Kidwelly, Llanelly and indeed the whole neighbourhood. Innuendo and suspicion in connection with Mabel Greenwood's death became so widespread that eventually the police became 'interested'.

On October 24th, 1919, shortly after Greenwood's return from honeymoon, he gave a lengthy statement when Police Supt. Jones and Inspector Nicholas of Llanelly, called at his office. During a second interview by the police on 31st October, Greenwood produced the death certificate. He was informed by them that in view of current rumours and people gossiping so freely, they would in all probability be applying for an exhumation of his wife's body. Greenwood's reply – "Just the very thing. I am quite agreeable."

The Chief Constable of Carmarthenshire, Mr Picton Phillips, submitted a long report to the Home Office on 9th March, 1920. He gave his opinion on the exhumation of Mrs Greenwood's body with these words – "Either in the interests of justice, or if that should happily not be so, then to relieve the husband of terrible suspicion, which will otherwise probably cling to him for life."

The Director of Public Prosecutions consulted the Coroner, J. W. Nicholas, and he recommended an unobtrusive watch be kept on Greenwood, in case he attempted to leave the country.

In April, the astounding news spread quickly that an Order had been issued by the Home Secretary for the exhumation of Mabel Greenwood's body, ten months after she had been laid to rest.

On 16th April, 1920, at dead of night the grave was opened with a posse of policemen standing guard (normal practice in such circumstances). The coffin was removed and taken to the mortuary at the

Kidwelly Town Hall where a post-mortem was conducted by Dr Alexander Dick in the morning. Relevant organs were removed from the body, placed in appropriate containers and sent by rail (GWR) to Dr John Webster, Government Analyst, Home Office. Ironically, the same railway station where Mabel Greenwood had caught a train to attend her tennis meeting in Ferryside.

Meanwhile, Harold Greenwood talked freely to the press – "I would not be surprised at all should arsenic or other poisons be found in my wife's body." At this stage no one had mentioned arsenic. Greenwood went on – "She never stopped taking medicines and potions, heaven knows what was in them all."

On June 8th, Chief Inspector Haigh of Scotland Yard commenced his enquiries into the mysterious death of Mabel Greenwood.

When the inquest re-opened on June 16th, 1920, excitement was at fever pitch. Dr William Henry Wilcox, a famous authority in his field, was asked – "Did your investigations reveal any signs of valvular heart disease, as stated on the death certificate?" Reply – "None whatsoever, sir." "Did you examine the organs?" "Yes, sir, arsenic was found in all the organs."

Chief Inspector Haigh.

Eighteen witnesses were examined, the Coroner's summing up lasted threequarters of an hour, and the jury of thirteen retired for thirty-five minutes. The verdict handed in by the foreman, Mr George Jones, was – "We are unanimously of the opinion that the death of the deceased Mabel Greenwood was caused by acute arsenic poisoning, as certified by Dr Wilcox, and that the poison was administered by Harold Greenwood."

Shortly afterwards, Harold Greenwood was seized by local policemen and charged on suspicion of having caused his wife's death by administration of poison. He was later taken to Llanelly Police Station and during the journey met with a great deal of hostility from bystanders.

On July 3rd, Greenwood was committed to the next Carmarthen Assizes, to stand trial on the above charge. He pleaded "Not guilty" and reserved his defence.

The stage was set for one of the country's most famous trials.

The trial itself aroused interest not only in Wales but also the whole country, as all Britain's eyes were fixed on a courtroom in Carmarthen where the impending fate of Harold Greenwood would be resolved.

The narrow streets of Carmarthen were thronged with a market-day crowd who stared at the carriage conveying Harold Greenwood from the Assize Court back to prison. The trial had deeply stirred all the Welsh countryside

A thorough search of Rumsey House and the adjoining stables and outbuildings took place prior to the trial; the police found a few bottles but there was no incriminating evidence on them or anywhere else. One arsenic source could have been through the purchase of a product from the local chemist – Clifford Jones (assistant to his father who was also a qualified chemist with a business in Bridge Street), said he had sold two tins of Weedicide to the prisoner on June 7th and 8th, 1919. These were delivered without secrecy and Greenwood had not even attempted to conceal the transaction.

Charles Dobson of Tomlinson and Hayward of Lincoln said that on April 22nd, 1919, a 100-gallon tin of Eureka Weedkiller was dispatched to Rumsey House. When questioned, he said there was about 60 per cent of arsenic in the product which was highly soluble.

Greenwood was held in Carmarthen gaol awaiting his trial for four and a half months.

THE TRIAL

The Guildhall, Carmarthen, venue of the trial, proved to be totally inadequate to accommodate the huge number of spectators in the

Crowds gather outside the court in Carmarthen for the trial of Harold Greenwood.
(Photograph courtesy Dr Terry James).

Miss Irene Greenwood (left) and Miss Eileen Greenwood, daughters
of the late Mrs Mabel Greenwood, arriving at the court.

courtroom during the proceedings. Consequently, the court was packed to suffocation point each day and there was an immense crowd waiting outside as well.

The poisoning mystery fired every Briton's imagination. Pressmen, representing all the daily papers descended on Carmarthen and even the American press were there. A good many silks found difficulty in obtaining rooms, as accommodation in the town had been fully booked several weeks in advance. Some witnesses had to be accommodated in Llanelly, and a journey to Carmarthen from Llanelly in the 1920s would have taken far longer than in these days of fast modern transport.

Mr Justice Shearman, the presiding Judge, arrived at Carmarthen on the Friday previous to the trial date. Accompanying him were his wife, Lady Shearman, and his son, Mr Montague Shearman, who acted as Judge's Marshall. Sir Edward Marlay Samson, KC, and Mr Wilfred Lewis appeared for the Crown. They would probably have been totally unnerved to learn who was defending Greenwood as he was just about the most clever and charismatic KC on the English legal scene, his name – Sir Edward Marshall Hall, KC. He was assisted by Mr Trevor Hunter, thereby acquiring for the defence the benefit of two outstanding barristers. Also in the courtroom was Mr Clark Williams, who held a watching brief on behalf of a certain interested party – a firm of weedkilling manufacturers.

Greenwood objected to three members of the jury who were consequently discharged. There was not a single jury person from Kidwelly.

These then were the principal figures who would act out one of the most famous trials in this country, and the trial went on for one whole week.

The trial opened on Tuesday, November 2nd, 1920. The Assize Calendar listed three cases of alleged murder and one of manslaughter, but the Greenwood trial overshadowed all the others.

Greenwood pleaded "Not Guilty" in answer to the charge against him.

The prosecution alleged that Mrs Greenwood's death was due to arsenic in the burgundy, purchased at the Phoenix off-licence, possibly placed whilst Greenwood was in the china pantry just before lunch on that fateful Sunday. Dr John Webster, a government analyst, was wielded in to give his opinion. Sir Edward Marlay Samson asked, "You saw Coopers Eureka Weedkiller, purchased by the accused, could it have caused death if dissolved in burgundy?"

Mr Justice Shearman, who had insisted that witnesses should not be addressed 'in a vehement way' by counsel.

Sir Edward Marlay Samson, KC.

Sir Edward Marshall Hall, KC.

"Yes, sir," was the reply. "I dissolved half a teaspoonful in a bottle of burgundy. A glassful of this would prove fatal, I was unable to taste the presence of poison in the wine, nor when I tried it in a cup of tea."

Marshall Hall interrupted – "Any particular blend of tea?"

The Judge rebuked him – "Really, Sir Edward."

Harold Greenwood sat cool and collected throughout the whole proceedings, even laughing on occasions. When he appeared in the witness box to be questioned by Marlay Samson, he remained cool and unruffled.

The opening speech delivered by Marlay Samson took two hours, during which time the witnesses were not present in court. Counsel then outlined three main points on which the jury had to make up their minds.

"First, did Mabel Greenwood die of arsenic poisoning? If they agreed she did, they must ask themselves – was the poison taken by herself, either voluntarily, or was it wilfully administered? If they decided that this last was the case, they must ask – did the prisoner give it to her?" Naturally, the Crown alleged that he had done so.

On the point of weedkiller, Counsel stated that it contained 60% of arsenic, and was easily dissolved in water, and, if in red wine, its similar colour, likewise any taste would be unnoticeable.

Cross-examined about his prescriptions: Dr T. R. Griffiths, the family doctor, who attended the late Mrs Greenwood in her last illness.

The medical evidence was consequently of the utmost importance. As we have seen the Crown sought to prove that Mabel Greenwood died of arsenic poisoning. But the Defence contended that she died from morphia poisoning, through an error on the part of Dr Griffiths who administered pills containing a dose of the latter drug, sufficient to cause death.

Marshall Hall concentrated his scorn and fury on the unfortunate Dr Griffiths. "Now, doctor, I put it to you that a fatal dose of arsenic would be some eight times that found by the Home Office Expert, Dr Wilcox, and I put it to you further doctor, that the cause of death in this case was the administration of two morphia pills by yourself."

"No, sir, opium they were, opium."

"I am afraid I did not catch that, doctor," snapped the Counsel.

"Opium pills, I gave Mrs Greenwood two pills of opium to allow her some rest, some sleep."

When Marshall Hall heard this change of evidence which contradicted the defence case, he began the first of the famous scenes which made the trial so notorious.

Dr Griffiths's evidence was hesitant and contradictory throughout and defence bombarded him with harrowing questions. On one occasion Counsel went so far as to suggest openly that the doctor, by what he described as a 'colossal blunder', had administered Fowlers solution of arsenic, instead of bismuth to Mrs Greenwood, as bottles containing both stood side by side in his surgery.

"No, sir, no," shouted the doctor.

The doctor failed to produce his prescription books, since as he had now retired, he said ". . . he had destroyed all his notes."

The Judge remarked here – "This was gross incompetence to have kept no medical records."

Marshall Hall renewed his attack with vigour and the Judge intervened, telling him to stop badgering the witness.

Counsel continued "But you stated in your deposition before the police that you supplied two morphia pills, I have a copy here."

"Opium sir, opium."

Marshall Hall's case all but vanished right then, he had a team of experts standing by to testify how powerful and lethal a drug morphia could be; suddenly it was no longer there and it made a nonsense of Hall's case.

One of the chief witnesses for the Crown was the parlour-maid Hannah Maggie Williams a nineteen year old who had worked at Rumsey House for nine months. She swore that at 12.30 p.m. on the fateful day, Greenwood entered the china pantry where the wine was stored and remained there for half an hour. She was hindered from laying the table for lunch, as the 'silver basket' was kept in the china pantry and she did not ". . . like to go in and

Miss Maggie Williams, a parlour-maid at Rumsey House.

fetch it while he was there." She declared she had never known him do this before. Greenwood stated, and witnesses were called to prove, that he constantly and frequently used the sink in the china pantry to wash his hands after washing the car or working in the garden. On this occasion he went in just as the gong sounded for dinner and did not remain there for more that a few minutes.

Hannah Williams was more familiar with speaking Welsh than English, and the Judge at times asked Marshall Hall to refrain from "shouting at" or "bullying" the witness. Nevertheless, *The Times*, in a leading article, called her evidence "hesitating and indefinite." When questioned with inaccuracy or contradiction of previous statements, her own admission that: "I cannot remember everything", was probably the stark truth.

Since her departure from Rumsey House, either voluntarily or because Greenwood following his wife's death did not retain her services, she had been employed by a Mrs Morris of Station Road, Kidwelly. Throughout her evidence, she stuck to her story that Greenwood spent at least half an hour in the china pantry on that particular Sunday and she had not known of him going there to wash his hands as a regular practice.

Hannah Williams laid the luncheon table and placed a bottle of burgundy in the place where Mrs Greenwood sat. A great deal of contradictory evidence arose concerning this. The young maid swore that she put it out on the table when laying the cloth for supper, and never saw it again. She looked for it in the sideboard the following day but could not find it. She went out on that Sunday evening at 5.30 p.m. and on her return the supper things had been taken away. Who by, she was unable to say. On her evening off duty, Irene Greenwood sometimes performed this task, but Hannah Williams did not know whether she had done so on this particular night, as Irene was much occupied with her mother's sudden illness. Hannah added: "It seems unlikely."

Irene Greenwood vowed that she drank burgundy at both lunch and supper on Sunday, June 15th, and asked Miss Phillips, a guest at the supper meal, to have wine, which she refused. Miss Phillips swore that she saw no wine of any kind on the supper table: ". . . as if there had been she would have had some." She saw whiskey down at the end where Greenwood sat, but definitely no wine.

Miss Margaret Ann Morris, employed as a cook in Rumsey House, under oath, said she: ". . . had been with the Greenwoods for over two years and they were a happy and affectionate couple. Mrs

Greenwood often had burgundy with her lunch." The witness also said: "Mr Greenwood often washed his hands in the china pantry after working in the garden."

Miss Gwyneira Powell, a housemaid at the Greenwood residence, said she: ". . . laid the table for luncheon the Sunday Mrs Greenwood was taken ill." She also said that Mrs Greenwood and Irene often took burgundy. Replying to Marlay Samson's cross-examination the witness, said that: "Hannah Williams remained in the dining room." Counsel asked – "So you would not have been there when they were having lunch or dinner?"

"No, sir."

He continued – "You simply put the bottle of burgundy on the table?"

"Yes."

The Crown called two expert witnesses to prove that arsenic had been administered. Dr John Webster, a Government Analyst, stated that approximately a quarter of a grain of arsenic was found in Mrs Greenwood's exhumed body. He found no morphine although it is possible that ten months after death this would have disappeared. The minimum fatal dose of arsenic was two grammes. On examining the weedkiller, Dr Webster found that it contained 55.6% of arsenic. When weedkiller was added to port wine, the colour was slightly altered he added.

Dr William Henry Wilcox, Home Office Pathologist, examined the organs which were in the possession of Dr Webster. He said cause of death was arsenical poisoning, definitely not a heart attack. His opinion as to the amount of arsenic in the body at the time of death, about threequarters to one grain. Despite extensive cross-examination by Marshall Hall, he maintained his opinion that arsenical poisoning caused the death.

Lieutenant Colonel F. S. Toogood, toxicologist to the London County Council, appearing for the defence, gave his opinion that Mrs Greenwood's death was due to morphia poisoning, following an attack of gastroenteritis, caused by swallowing gooseberry skins.

Marlay Samson's cross-examination of this witness elicited a good many facts, which tended to weaken the effect of Dr Toogood's evidence.

Dr William Griffiths of Swansea contended for the defence and said that finding a quarter of a grain of arsenic in the viscera of a dead body was not conclusive evidence that it had been the cause of death. He also thought Mrs Greenwood died of morphia poisoning.

*The original Welsh sideboard, showing the cellaret
where wine and spirits were kept.*
(Photograph courtesy Mr Neville Jones).

*Mr Harold Greenwood himself
went into the witness box before
his daughter Irene and was
questioned for four hours.*

Defence produced several theories to account for the small quantity of arsenic found in the body. No firm conclusion as to what caused the death of Mabel Greenwood was ever really arrived at. Arsenical poisoning, morphine poisoning, her weak condition worsened by eating gooseberries – the question remains open to this day.

On the fifth day of the trial Harold Greenwood faced Sir Edward Marlay Samson for cross-examination. Counsel raised two issues regarding the night of Mabel Greenwood's death – "As your wife's condition became considerably worse, you were sent by the nurse to fetch Dr Griffiths, and were so long in returning with or without him, that your daughter Irene had to go to the doctor's home, to discover the reason for this delay." Greenwood swore that he had not been more than ten minutes, an opinion later endorsed by Miss Mary Griffiths. However, Miss Phillips and Nurse Jones both agreed he was away for nearly an hour. Still later, when his wife was practically at the point of death, Greenwood was urged to bring Dr Griffiths, but came back alone, saying – "I could not rouse him." The nurse went over and wakened the doctor at once.

The prosecution made much of these two incidents as emphasising Greenwood's conduct was highly inconsistent with his 'supposed' anxiety about his wife.

Marlay Samson continued cross-examination –

"Were you very attached to your wife at the time of her death?"

"Yes."

"She died on June 16th?"

"Yes."

"On July 4th did you buy a diamond ring?"

"I wrote for it on July 4th and bought it on July 11th."

"Whom did you give the ring to?"

"I bought if for my daughter in the first instance."

"That is not the answer to my question, I asked to whom did you give the ring?"

"Eventually, I gave it to Miss Gladys Jones."

"Was that about on July 27th?"

"Yes, about then."

"Though you had a great affection for your wife, a month after her death you gave Miss Jones a diamond ring, for which you paid £55."

Greenwood's answer was inaudible.

Although Greenwood did not marry Miss Jones until October 1st, he proposed within a month of his wife's death and the ring was obviously ordered as an engagement ring.

Mrs Groves, caretaker/cleaner at Greenwood's office in Llanelly, testified to finding the remains of a partially burnt letter in the grate at the office, which she believed to be in Gladys Jones's handwriting. In the letter were the words, 'It will be nice when I am your wife'. The receipt for the diamond ring was also found by the cleaner – discarded as waste paper. Mrs Groves also alleged that Miss Jones often visited Greenwood in his office.

The defence made much of the fact that Greenwood was depen-dant on his wife's private income of around £700 a year – a lot of money in those days. Income from Greenwood's law practice varied greatly from year to year. Mabel Greenwood's death saw payments from her father's estate stop, and a major part of their income lost.

Police Sergeant Hodge Lewis of Kidwelly said under oath that he supervised the exhumation of the body of Mrs Greenwood and the sealing of the jars containing organs taken from the body.

Sgt. Lewis, cross-examined by Marshall Hall was asked – "Did you interview a man called Benjamin Williams?" Reply was "yes."

"Was this in consequence of something said, that the man who knew everything about the weedkiller was Williams?" "Yes," he replied.

Sgt. Lewis then read a long statement from his notebook in which Williams said: ". . . he assisted in sprinkling weedkiller on the path. The weedkiller would be mixed in large tins holding about four gallons." But Williams said he never saw the weedkiller being used by Greenwood.

Reading from his much discussed notebook: Superintendent Samuel Jones.

Police Supt. Jones of Llanelly entered the witness box to be cross-examined by Marshall Hall who suggested that the statement in the police witness notebook was not that written at the actual interview with Greenwood but copied afterwards. The witness denied this allegation.

Counsel then asked – "Has this book had any pages taken out?"

"None whatsoever," was the reply.

Counsel continued – "Check that book again; have pages been torn out?"

"No," was the reply.

The notebook was then handed to the jury, each of whom examined it minutely. Marshall Hall continued – "I am not suggesting that this gent tore pages out but a leaf has been removed from the book."

Counsel then compared the notebook with a new one of police issue.

He then asked the witness – "Can you say under oath that no pages have been taken out; remember, a man is on trial here for his life."

The officer insisted – "No pages have been taken out."

The result of allegations that pages which contained some of the statements had been torn out of the notebook led to an interesting development. These facts were strenuously denied, but in consequence of this case the police implemented the current practice of numbering every page of police notebooks.

Sir Edward Marshall Hall, great advocate that he was, had another ace up his sleeve. A young twenty-one year old governess was called to the witness box.

Miss Irene Greenwood.

Counsel began – "You are employed as a governess in London?"

"Yes, sir."

"And you are?"

"Irene Greenwood, sir, daughter of the accused."

"Now take your time, Miss Greenwood, and tell the court about luncheon on Sunday, June 15th, last year. What did you have to drink?"

"The same as mother, sir, a glass of burgundy."

There were gasps of amazement around the courtroom.

Hall had pulled the carpet from under the prosecution's feet.

Irene Greenwood was the last witness called for the defence. She brought the case to an end, by her declaration under oath that on the fateful Sunday she drank twice from the bottle alleged to contain poison.

Sir Edward Marlay Samson made the point that wine was not the only liquid drunk by Mrs Greenwood within twelve hours of her death. She had taken tea, brandy and medicine, any of which might have contained poisonous weedkiller. But he was clutching at straws.

At the conclusion of Irene Greenwood's evidence, the Judge stated he was adjourning until 10 o'clock on the Monday morning.

On Monday, November 8th, 1920, very large crowds occupied both inside and outside the Guildhall. Inside, the packed courtroom awaited the summing up speeches of both Counsels.

The *South Wales Press* described how Sir Edward Marshall Hall's speech took up the morning session: "The famous KC used all his faculties to the utmost to overcome his disposition (he had been ill throughout the trial). How far he succeeded may be judged from the fact that he reached his own highest level of forensic eloquence in the closing passage of his speech."

He contrasted and compared the achievements of science with that great miracle of life, which science could not achieve. "Inferences from Science," called Sir Edward, "can be drawn by which a man may forfeit his life, but once that tiny spark which turns a mass of clay into a sentient human being is quenched, there are no means known to science by which it may be lit again."

In a moment of high emotional drama, Sir Edward quoted Shakespear's 'Othello'. Referring to that part in the play when Othello found Desdemonia lying asleep in bed, Sir Edward quoted a lengthy passage and in the most moving terms concluded – "I know not where is the Promethean heat which can thy light return."

When he referred to Irene Greenwood in the witness box, Greenwood was overcome with emotion and bent his grey head.

"Would you hang a cat on evidence like this?" Sir Edward exclaimed a little later.

In a terribly graphic passage, he warned each juryman that he must be so sure of Greenwood's guilt, that he could say – "If that man were standing on the executioner's platform, I myself would draw the lever that hurls him into eternity."

Finally, he concluded – "I demand at your hands the life and liberty of Harold Greenwood."

Sir Edward Marlay Samson's summing up lasted for three hours. As the *South Wales Press* stated:

> "His address, which was a model of the analytical method, was an appeal to logic and reason. He paid splendid homage to Sir Edward but in his calm, measured tones, declared that the case for the Crown was not a matter for oratory but for scientific investigation.
>
> "He said that Greenwood desired Gladys Jones, and to consummate that desire made away with his wife. The most thrilling part of his speech was delivered in the deepening dusk, when he pleaded for justice for the poor soul who lies in Kidwelly churchyard."

In his brief address to the jury the Judge warned them not to be influenced in their discussions by:

> "Fear of a lurid picture of a condemned man on the gallows."

"Fear of deciding on a verdict that might be unpopular."

"Being prejudiced because there were things about Green-wood which they might not like."

The Judge, Mr Justice Shearman, finished his summing up and the jury retired at 1.23 p.m. The jury were away for only a brief interval.

The Judge took his seat again at 3.53 p.m., as night gathered in the gloomy, gaslit courtroom.

Then Kidwelly's ghosts came crowding back, not to be laid to rest, even to this day.

Let the *South Wales Press* reporter at the trial describe the scene:

"There was a great hush. The feelings of the people who were witnesses, of what had been looked upon as the greatest poisoning mystery of modern times, had been aroused to a nerve wrecking degree of tension, and one could almost hear heart beats in the silence of the last few moments. At 3.55 p.m. Greenwood re-appeared and he immediately set his eyes with a fixed stare at the jury. He was naturally labouring under great excitement, and seemed to be trying to read his fate in the face of the foreman of the Jury."

When the Judge turned to the jury, Greenwood focused his attention on his lordship.

A moment later, the Hon. Stephen Coleridge said – "Gentlemen of the Jury, have you agreed upon a verdict?"

The foreman: "Yes, My Lord."

The Hon. Stephen Coleridge – "Look upon the prisoner at the bar, and say whether he is guilty or not guilty."

The foreman, obeying the instructions, turned his eyes toward Greenwood, and in calm deliberate tones, uttered the dramatic words: "Not Guilty."

There were some cheers, clapping, but also a fair amount of booing.

So, Harold Greenwood was free, or was he? The jury handed in a written rider to their verdict, not read out in court at the time, but soon became public knowledge. It read:

"We are satisfied on the evidence in this case that a dangerous dose of arsenic was administered to Mabel Greenwood on Sunday, June 15th, 1919, but we are not satisfied that this was the immediate cause of death.

The evidence before us is insufficient, and does not con-
clusively satisfy us as to how, and by whom, the arsenic was
administered. We therefore return a verdict of 'Not Guilty'."

In a Scottish court this could have been recorded as a "Not
Proven" verdict – here it said – we known he did it but cannot prove
it to any gossips in Kidwelly.

Harold Greenwood may have been free but he was ruined; his
practice gone, what little money he had was lost to the enormous
costs of Marshall Hall's defence and his health ravaged by strain.

There is no doubt that had not Harold Greenwood rushed into a
second marriage, he would not have appeared in the Assize charged
with murder. The motive for his second marriage took up much time
at the trial, and the arguments, as with the medical evidence, played
a part in the end to influence the jury in their deliberations.

Innocent of murder but guilty of quick re-marriage or philandering!

So Harold Greenwood changed his name and vanished, or nearly
so, into the annals of history.

What did really happen? Did Mabel Greenwood die of arsenical
poisoning, morphia poisoning, or was it natural causes?

Who spoke the truth under oath? Irene Greenwood who swore
that she had drunk burgundy at lunch and supper, or Miss Phillips
who swore there was no wine on the supper table. Hannah Williams
who swore Greenwood was in the china pantry for half and hour or
the accused who swore he was only in there for a few minutes.

All in all, nothing could help Mabel Greenwood or the family and
sadly they vanished from the stage.

Mabel's remains were re-buried in St Mary's churchyard in some
haste and in secrecy, in order to avoid 'gawpers'. We will probably
never know what happened to the children.

Though a most touching memorial to her father came from Harold's
eldest daughter, Irene, whose testimony saved his life.

"Daddy was always very good to us, we were always together" –
Pathetic epitaph for a Mr .... Pilkington, who died of cancer age 54,
on the 17th January 1929 in Herefordshire.

1922 Waxworks Effigy
In Cardiff on 9th March, 1922, there was an echo of Harold Greenwood's trial. Mr D'Arc, a waxworks proprietor in Cardiff, had displayed a wax figure of Mr Greenwood in an inappropriate zone of
his exhibition, and therefore Mr Greenwood cited libel charges
against him claiming damages.

The unmarked grave of Mabel Greenwood, 2003.
(Photograph: Author).

Mr Artemus Jones KC (Counsel for Mr Greenwood) told the court that Mr D'Arc's exhibition was divided into three categories –

1. Biblical characters.
2. Various celebrities, such as prime ministers, popes, etc.
3. Chamber of Horrors.

Even though Mr Greenwood had been acquitted of the murder charge in November 1920, Mr D'Arc had taken it upon himself to exploit the notoriety of the Greenwood trial. He had displayed Harold Greenwood's wax figure alongside effigies of convicted murderers in the Chamber of Horrors, obviously for financial gain.

Mr Greenwood entered the witness box, white haired and neatly attired in a navy-blue suit.

The judge found for Mr Greenwood and he was awarded £150 damages.

With the exception of those marked, all photographs and sketches in this chapter are from 'Scrapbook Greenwood Case – Sir Edward Marlay Samson – 2nd November, 1920'.

5

Notable Events

1103-1112 Royal Charter
Some time between the years 1103 and 1112 Henry I granted the first
Kidwelly Charter to Roger, Bishop of Salisbury, Lord of Kidwelly.

1210 – Royal Visitor
Kidwelly has been graced by visits from reigning monarchs on several
occasions, King John in 1210 being the first royal visitor to the town.

May 1313 – Ancient Document
Written in Norman French the earliest document held in Carmarthen
Records Office is a 'Grant regarding fishing rights in the River Towy'
given at Kidwelly Castle, on the tenth day of May, in the sixth year
of the reign of Edward II (10th May, 1313).

1516 – Lord Mayor of London
Many notable Welshmen claim their place of birth to be 'Ye Ancient
Boro of Cydweli', but there is no doubt that Sir John Yarford, a native
of Kidwelly, did become Lord Mayor of London in 1516 – a local
Dick Whittington.

1830 – Clockmaker and Town Crier
Evan Davies, Clock and Watch maker, worked in Causeway Street,
Kidwelly, later Bridge Street and New Street, between 1830-1875.
He was also the Town Crier and appears in the 1851 census age 53.
He manufactured eight-day longcase grandfather clocks, many with
painted dials of local scenes. A lathe used by him can be seen in a
collection (No. 45.68) at the Museum of Welsh Life at St Fagan's in
Cardiff, having been donated in 1945. The museum also possesses a
slip of paper featuring Davies of Kidwelly (No. 61.9.1) which is in
fact a small advertisement placed inside the watch-case by the makers,
in this instance Davies of Kidwelly. The paper bears a picture of Old

Father Time holding an hourglass and scythe with the words Davies/ Clock/and Watch/Maker/Kidwelly on it. A memorial to Evan Davies can be seen etched on a plaque attached to the west wall above the font inside St Mary's Church.

May 1871 – Flags

As was the custom, an annual treat was given the scholars of the Kidwelly British School by Jacob Chivers of Velindre House on Whit Monday. On one such day over 200 children marched from the town to Velindre, located to the north-west of the town (now called the Gwenllian Court Hotel) and were given tea with a plentiful supply of cakes. Later on in the day, they played games in an adjoining field and in the evening they assembled at the front of the mansion and sang several songs. Mrs Evans, of Rumsey House, kindly presented each child with a flag.

August 1871 – Croquet

The diaries of Agnes Jennings of Gellydeg in the Parish of Llandefeilog, recalls a dance held in the grounds of Kidwelly Castle: "It was a beautiful day, there were 50 to 60 people present, we dined in the inner court, Jones's band played. Later we played croquet in the outer court and then we had tea."

March 1894 – Fever Hospital

At a Council Meeting, the Mayor Ald. D. Stephens of the Arlais and the Medical Officer Dr Jones agreed that a site suitable for the proposed Fever Hospital had been found accessible and available at the town quay.

Proposed site for the Fever Hospital at the Quay. Early 1960s.
(Photograph courtesy Peter Evans).

January 1902 – New Year Gifts

On New Year's Day, as has been the custom for several years, Mr and Mrs Alexander Young of Glanmorfa, gave to 100 of the poorer families in Kidwelly, a large quantity of tea, sugar and bread. Some 800 children also received one penny and some biscuits.

Old Town Bridge and Trinity Chapel. Late 1800s.
(Photograph courtesy Kidwelly Town Council).

Old Town Bridge and Bridge Street. Early 1900s.
(Photograph courtesy Peter Evans).

June 1911 – Bridge Widening
A major undertaking was in progress, i.e. widening of the medieval town bridge that spanned the Gwendraeth Fach River. The narrow bridge had become a traffic hazard and the work was proceeding,

as part of the old bridge had already been demolished to make room for the new foundations.

December 1911 – Ancient Bridge
Widening of the town bridge was near completion. The improvement had become essential as the ancient bridge was no longer strong enough to take the volume of traffic that passed over it.

September 1922 – Memorial Tablet
On a Sunday evening in September 1922 a marble memorial tablet bearing the names of 39 brave men who fell in the Great War was

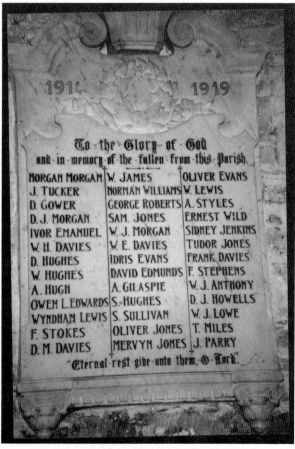

Memorial Tablet in St Mary's Church, 2003.
(Photograph: Author).

unveiled and dedicated by the Vicar, Rev. D. Ambrose Jones M.A., and the Rev. Owen Phillips M.A., Vicar of Haverfordwest. The restored figure of Madonna and Child which had previously occupied a niche above the entrance door of the church, was now displayed in a space above the new memorial tablet. A large congregation attended the ceremony and the church was tastefully decorated for the occasion. Captain D. Brynmor Anthony M.A., M.C. – a local 'boy' – who was awarded the Military Cross for heroism during his war time service – read the Roll of Honour. The organist was Mr D. Thomas and Miss Queenie Price sang a solo.

May 1923 – Eisteddfod in Castle

In May 1923 the War Memorial Committee held an eisteddfod in the castle, which proved to be a great success and a good fund-raiser. Presidents for the day were H. E. Smart, Mountain View in the morning, John Hinds, M.P. of Carmarthen in the afternoon and Alderman S. H. Anthony, Mayor of Kidwelly in the evening.

July 1923 – Knighthood

The residents of Kidwelly were loud in their appreciation when news reached the town of the knighthood of Sir Alfred Stephens JP, of Broomhill. All the streets were bedecked with flags and the bells of St Mary's Church rang joyfully to mark the occasion. The Silica Brick-works was decorated with bunting and flags were hoisted to fly high. The whole of the workforce showed their approval and delight by turning out to greet him and singing 'For he's a jolly good fellow'. Sir Alfred expressed his appreciation and declared a general holiday at which news there was even louder cheering.

July 1936 – 16th Century Ring

Mrs S. Busst, the popular custodian of the castle, was presented with a photograph of a gold signet ring which had been found during excavation work at the fortress. It was believed that Sir John Digby, 1533, had been the owner of the ring, which is now in the custody of the British Museum, Department of Medieval Antiquities.

April 1937 – War Shrine

Miss James of the Barbican presented the first war shrine in Kidwelly, which hung on the outside walls of St Mary's Church. The shrine, carved in wood, was now weather beaten and beyond repair, and in

1937 there was no alternative but to remove it. There were two other war memorials in the town – one was a tablet attached to a wall inside the church and the other a superb construction in New Street.

June 1937 – Rare Coin

While digging in his garden Mr Fred Menghetti of Ferry Road found what was later identified to be a very rare coin. On closer examination it was found to be a half noble of Richard II, 1377-99 era, and there were very few in existence.

July 1937 – Silver Salver

A special function was held at the Pelican Hotel when Sir Alfred Stephens was presented with a solid silver salver to mark the high esteem in which he was held by his employees. Chairman of the Works Committee, Mr David Rees of Llansaint, presided.

August 1937 – First Carnival

The first ever carnival and sports event was held at Park Stephens one Saturday in August and full credit to John Jones of The Grove for organising the event. All the takings would increase funds being raised towards the cost of erecting a new Public Hall and Institute. Carnival queen, who was also coronation queen, was Miss Irene Sheppard of Broomhill Cottages.

October 1938 – Harrods

Mr Tom Anthony, Managing Director of the famous Harrods London store, native of Kidwelly, sent one thousand books for use in Kidwelly Library and Institute. This was the second time Mr Anthony had made a donation of books. He was a generous benefactor who despite his success in the business world, had not forgotten the town of his birth.

1942 – Dig for Victory

During the Second World War, the Government issued a series of 'Dig for Victory' leaflets as an aid to the war effort. The leaflets were produced by the Ministry of Agriculture based at St Annes-on-Sea in Lancashire, and encouraged people to grow their own crops as a contribution to the national effort on food production. People were prompted to dig their gardens and allotments with hints ranging from how to dig, harvesting and storing, how to deal with pests, how to make a compost heap, drying, salting, etc. etc. Many of these leaflets have survived the tide of time – I was shown a few by a friend in Mynydd-y-Garreg.

DIG FOR VICTORY   LEAFLET No. 5

CABBAGES AND RELATED CROPS

THE cabbage family can provide food from the garden in all seasons of the year—highly nutritious food, particularly rich in protective vitamins.

Spring, autumn, red and savoy cabbages, kales or borecole, Brussels sprouts, broccoli and cauliflower should be in every garden and allotment, but it is important to remember that they are more perishable than most crops ; they must be consumed in a freshly gathered condition.

To avoid waste, therefore, grow no more of each than is sufficient for the family's needs. Plan the cropping of these important vegetables so that valuable garden space is not taken up by surplus produce.

CABBAGES

For Spring and Early Summer Cutting

Early Offenham, Wheeler's Imperial and *Ellams Early* are suitable either for cutting when the plants are semi-hearted or when solid hearts have developed.

Flower of Spring is a later variety, making a large plant. It can, however be cut as spring greens.

For Late Summer and Autumn Cutting

Winningstadt is a good late summer cabbage. *Primo*, which is of dwarf habit, making few outer leaves and developing solid, round-shaped heads, can be planted closer together in the rows than some types.

Stockley's Giant Red is excellent for pickling purposes. Red cabbages are the most suitable for pickling, but can also be eaten as a fresh vegetable.

For Winter Cutting

January King and *Christmas Drumhead* are hardy types.

SAVOYS

Best of All is grown for cutting in early winter, and *Ormskirk Late* is suitable for cutting in March and April. Savoys are very hardy, with curled and puckered leaves. On account of their flavour they are often preferred to cabbages.

BRUSSELS SPROUTS

This crop is the chief source of supply of fresh, green food for late autumn and winter. When arranging a plan of cropping for the garden, space should be allowed to accommodate a fair-sized plot of sprouts. Although there are many varieties, a good mid-season type will suffice. Either *Harrison's XXX* or *Evesham Giant* will be suitable, but for persons with very limited space a dwarf sort such as *Dwarf Gem* is to be preferred.

(Copy of leaflet courtesy Mr Morgan Davies).

Signpost, 2003.
(Photograph: Author).

March 1965 – Welcome Signs
Kidwelly was the first town in Carmarthenshire to erect 'Welcome' signs on its boundaries. The idea was triggered off by the Borough Council's Industries Committee and the signs were installed on all five roads leading into the town. The borough's crest, viz a black cat, is displayed at the centre of the signpost with the words 'Welcome to Kidwelly, founded 1115' inserted underneath.

August 1965 – Illuminated Clock
As their contribution to the movements jubilee celebrations, Kidwelly Women's Institute made arrangements to illuminate the clock on the tower of the town's 13th century church of St Mary. Mrs Beryl Evans, the Institute's President, said that the cost of the illuminations would be met by the Mayor, Cllr. Vincent Thomas, who said a separate meter would be installed and the council would pay for the electricity consumed.

September 1966 – Historic Moment
Kidwelly citizens have chosen a woman to be Mayor Elect of the borough for the very first time in its 850-year history. Cllr. Miss Charlotte Squire stood as an Independent member of the Council, held the esteemed rank of Commandant of the Kidwelly Red Cross Detachment, and served as Secretary on the Old People's Welfare Committee.

April 1969 – Buckingham Palace
Kidwelly took its fight to keep the 860 years old Borough Charter to London, where copies of a petition bearing 3,000 signatures, were handed in at Buckingham Palace, at 10 Downing Street, the Welsh Office and the House of Commons at Westminster.

It was the last task undertaken by Ald. Henry John Owen, the retiring Mayor prior to the hand-over of office to his successor. Accompanying him on his 'Save-the-Borough' mission was town Clerk Mr Ernald Jones. In London, they were met by Carmarthenshire's M.P. Mr Gwynfor Evans who stayed with them and supported them at hand-over of the petitions. In the local government reshuffle due to take place in 1972, Kidwelly was one of four constituent authorities intended to be merged into a 'greater Llanelli'. The petition sought retention of the borough's ancient rights, privileges and boundaries, and that the authority should not lose its identity to a larger council. Kidwelly had sustained its status of borough since 1112, and at one time held its own Quarter and Petty Sessions and Commission of the Peace.

1973 – Thrilling Discovery
The discovery of a squint, also known as an hagioscope, in St Mary's Church during restoration activities in 1973 was very exciting. The hagioscope is an oblique shaped cavity formed through the wall, in this case between the vicar's vestry and the chancel, affording a view of the High Altar from the vestry. There appears to be no reference to the hagioscope in any document or historical record of the church prior to its discovery. This is not surprising as it had been concealed in the wall and well covered with thick plaster almost certainly since the 1530s. The extant records date from 1586, so it was exposed to the light of day, in all probability for the first time in almost 500 years, when the channel was uncovered. The Rev. Douglas Walters, incumbent at the time, stated – "The workmen were removing plaster on

Hagioscope as seen from the High Altar, St Mary's Church, 2003
(Photograph: Author).

the chancel wall when they discovered what appeared to be a picture frame. They cleared the rubble and found an angular cavity through the wall. It was very exciting, especially when we uncovered the other end of the squint in the vicar's vestry. It was quite thrilling to be able to see the altar from the vestry." There was a suggestion that possibly the hagioscope was walled up at the time of the Dissolution of the Monasteries in the mid-1530s, during the reign of Henry VIII.

1979 – Fleur-de-Lis

An important discovery linking the church with its mediaeval past was made in St Mary's Church by craftsmen working for the Rev. Douglas Walters in 1979. Two large stone memorial slabs of the 19th century which had become unsafe were removed from above the entrance to the chancel vestry. Subsequently, a large plaque bearing a decorative motif of the fleur-de-lis was revealed. Canon Walters explained the significance of the ornamental art motif – "In mediaeval times the fleur-de-lis was accepted in France as the emblem of the Virgin Mary. It was usually found on the northern wall of the church, as here at St Mary's. Its traditional link with the Arms of France and the Flemings cannot be questioned.

July 1988 – Royal Visit
Prince Charles received a truly royal welcome when he arrived at Kidwelly Industrial Museum, to the sound of the National Anthem being sung by local schoolchildren. He was taken on a guided tour of the Museum by Bill Morris, Chairman of the Tinplate Museum Trust, Miss Freda Phillips, Museum Chairman, and Susan Thomas, Curator. The Prince met Mrs Margaret Ann Morgan, 96 years of age, who started working at the Tin Plate Works when she was just 13 years old. Mrs Morgan was born in a cottage situated just behind the tin plate works and had lived there all her life.

Town Bridge over the Gwendraeth Fach river, 2003.
(Photograph: Author).

6

Unusual Occurrences and Oddities

March 1738 – Missing Cockerel
A weathercock was installed on top of the church steeple at a cost of five guineas. It was forged in copper, measured 6 feet from the point of its beak to the tip of its tail and weighed over a hundredweight. It was blown off its perch during a severe gale in 1845 and mysteriously disappeared shortly after.

February 1866 – Concert Uproar
A concert held at the British Schoolroom ended in uproar when trio Town Mayor Cllr. Braithwayte, MC, Mr Evans of Rumsey House, and soloist Mrs Beynon of the Kidwelly Choral Society, almost came to blows because of a disagreement concerning the encore.

February 1871 – Endurance Challenge
Mr Samuel Richards claimed to be the local champion endurance skipper, challenged any Kidwelly or Mynydd-y-Garreg man to a skipping match of endurance. He was prepared to put up cash as a side bet.

November 1878 – Giant Pumpkin
Two huge pumpkins were grown by David Davies of China Warehouse, Tin Works Road, Kidwelly. The larger of the two measured 5ft 10 inches in circumference and weighed over a hundredweight.

November 1889 – Capture of a Monster Fish in Kidwelly
On Sunday, November 28th, 1889, a very large dead fish was discovered in the Gwendraeth Fach River, just below the town bridge. It had become trapped by some timbers lying at the water's edge, probably the cause of its demise. Conveyed by horse and cart, the fish was taken to a local farmhouse where large numbers of people called by to see the unusual visitant.

On Saturday evening, the fish it seems, had been seen swimming

'Tunny' PB03.

around in the Gwendraeth Fawr River, close to Commissioners Bridge.

On Monday morning it was taken to the Pelican Hotel where a charge was raised for entry to see this remarkable specimen. From snout to tip of tail it measured 9 feet 8 inches in length and about 7 feet around its girth. Opinions varied as to its breed but eventually ascertained to be 'Tunny' or 'Thunnus' fish, native of the Mediterranean Sea.

The 'Thunnus Tynnus' is the picturesque 'titan of tunas' and can reach a length of 14 feet and a weight of 1,800 lbs.

November 1893 – Ancient Oak

Construction of a new railway bridge over the Gwendraeth Fach river had commenced and three tubes had already been sunk into the riverbed. In their line of duty, construction workers using one of the tubes set about twenty feet below the river, discovered the trunk of an oak tree, which was likely to have been there for hundreds, possibly thousands of years. A comment was made that it would be well worthwhile preserving such an offbeat curio.

1900s – 'Hoelion Rhew'

Horses and carts were the means whereby stone was transported from Mynydd-y-Garreg quarries to the Tinplate Works and the Brickworks in Kidwelly. When hard frosts threatened in winter, blacksmiths fitted the horses with ice nails (*hoelion rhew*) on their hooves to serve as spikes which would provide a grip on slippery surfaces. Persistent roadwork caused the hooves to become badly worn, at which time the horses would be retired early and sold off to local farmers; many lived to a ripe old age.

December 1906 – The Missing Railway Fireman

Mr Howard Richards of Maes-ar-ddafan Road in Llanelli, who died in 1963, aged 85, spent 44 years on the footplate with the G.W.R. A fine record. It was, however, for another reason that Mr Richards was principally remembered by his former colleagues. Indeed, during his lifetime, he acquired legendary status among the railwaymen of Britain. His story harks back to a Christmas night, stormy and thick with sleet, in the year 1906, when he was the fireman on the 6 p.m. mail train from Neyland to Paddington. As the train travelled at between 60-70 m.p.h. on the coastal stretch between Ferryside and Kidwelly, Mr Richards crossed the rocking floor of the engine to replace the pricker – a long-handled rake – on the tender. He was

reaching out towards the tender when a mighty gust of wind caught the implement and took it over the side of the engine. Mr Richards still holding on to it, went overboard with it.

The engine driver, a Mr Frank Downing of Llanelli, was at the time peering ahead into the darkness and did not see it happen. It was not until the train was on the Kidwelly outskirts that he became aware he was alone on the footplate. At Kidwelly, where he stopped to report the disappearance of his mate, a porter was pressed into service to act as fireman until the train reached Llanelli. Mr Downing carried on as far as Landore, but then had become so upset by the disappearance of his fireman that he was relieved of duty. Meanwhile, much was going on in Kidwelly. A down-line express was halted and a search party, on a hand-propelled trolley, set out to recover the remains of the missing fireman.

The searchers met Mr Richards walking calmly alongside the track, the rake carried 'at the slope' over a shoulder. He had, he said, found himself in a pool in a field. All the clothes on one side had been stripped off him as he plunged clear of the track from the footplate. He was not unscathed. He had a head injury and a sore arm, but the doctor who examined him opined that ". . . he could not have received less hurt if he had pitched from the engine on to a feather bed." All things considered, Mr Richards could be reckoned to have since lived 56 years on 'borrowed' time.

July 1912 – Explosion

A treacherous act of cowardice took place in the early hours of one Sunday morning at Pendre when the cottage of labourer Thomas Williams was almost destroyed by an explosion of dynamite or some other such bomb. The device was planted under the front doorstep and when detonated the front door blew in and all the windows in the house, as well as the adjacent house, were smashed to smithereens. Fortunately, there was no other damage. Williams and his wife and two children were in the house and tucked up in bed at the time. The cottage was capped with a thatched roof, and the headroom was low, typical of some of the scant structures designed in those days. Amazingly, the roof did not ignite even though the thatch was tinder dry.

June 1915 – Circus Loss

The visiting Sir Robert Fossett circus suffered the loss of a valuable thoroughbred black performing horse called Napoleon in unusual circumstances. Along with several others, the horse was taken to the river to be washed and groomed, and somehow Napoleon strayed into deep water and was drowned. The horse, one of the best known in the circus business was valued at £175.

February 1922 – Early Car Accident
The Rev. W. C. Jenkins, Minister of Capel Sul, was knocked down by a motor car in Causeway Street but he was very fortunate to have suffered only severe shock and bruising. The incident was a most unusual occurrence as there were very few cars in the town. The car pulled up and the remorseful driver took the shaken Rev. Jenkins to his home in Ferry Road.

February 1923 – Floor Collapse
A very large crowd had gathered to attend the sale conducted by W. D. James, Auctioneer, at 7 West End Terrace when the floor in one of the rooms gave way and the auctioneer and several prospective buyers dropped into a cavity 5-6 ft deep. Fortunately, there were no serious injuries but the incident created a great deal of excitement. The sale did proceed – this time in the safety of the open air!

June 1934 – Farm on Wheels
A huge exercise was taken in hand when Mr and Mrs James Morris of Gardde Isaf moved by rail the whole of their farm, lock, stock and barrel, from Kidwelly to Grange Farm at Great Linford in Buckinghamshire. Newport Pagnell, on the London, Midland and Scottish line, was the nearest railway station to Great Linford and the Great Western Railway (GWR) ran a special train of 14 vehicles (two trucks for furniture, six trucks for livestock, five trucks for implements, and one passenger coach for all the family and farmhands – ten people in all).

It was necessary for the transfer to be completed between two milkings, so the cows were milked, herded to the railway station and loaded onto the train in the afternoon, leaving Kidwelly at 7.15 p.m. on Wednesday, 13th June. The convoy arrived at Newport Pagnell at 6.30 a.m. on Thursday morning, 14th June, where arrangements were in place to reach Grange Farm by road on the last lap of the journey, so the cows were walked a couple of miles to the farm, they were milked and before 8 a.m. a lorry arrived to collect the milk.

A large number of enthusiastic well wishers had gathered at Kidwelly Railway Station to witness the departure and as the train

chugged slowly away, a hearty cheer was raised in salute to the migrating family.

Mrs Mair Protheroe, one of the Morris's five children, 12 years old at the time, recalls that half the town was there at the station, all the schoolchildren were there as well, and a very emotional occasion it was with many of the waving party, and those on the train also, in tears. As the train left Kidwelly, Mair remembers that all the people from outlying farms had walked the fields alongside the railway line to wave greetings and good wishes.

February 1925 – Town Bridge Under Water
Flood water played havoc when it gushed down from the hills above Ferry Road turning the surge into a turbulent river several feet deep. The road was churned up and strewn with tons of boulders and other debris. Some of the houses in New Street were flooded to a depth of three feet and for the first time in living memory the town bridge over the Gwendraeth Fach River became impassable. Roads in other parts of the town became flooded by reason of the severe storm as well, and workmen on their way to the Tinplate Works had to be conveyed by boat on a stretch of road between Gwendraeth Farm and the hamlet of Llangadog to reach their place of work.

1944 – Ghosts
People who lived at or near Newtown in Mynydd-y-Garreg during the war would regularly seek shelter in the lime kilns during air raids. On one occasion, a bomb landed half a mile away – near to Rogerley

Farm – which on impact with the ground, shook the whole area including the kilns. When the group eventually emerged from the kilns, there was hearty laughter (characteristic Welsh reaction) all round, as they looked like a bunch of indiscernible ghosts covered as they were from head to toe in white lime.

January 1947 – Heavy Snowfall
The heaviest snowfall in living memory caused blizzard conditions to prevail in the town. Strong winds whipped up the snow to form massive drifts and the town was cut off from the outside world for over a week. The Arctic-like weather conditions continued for several weeks which caused real hardship for the inhabitants of the town and especially for people who lived in the outlying villages.

January 1963 – Arctic Weather
The heaviest snowfall since 1947, sub-zero temperatures and Arctic weather conditions caused the whole area to be buried under a blanket of deep snow. High winds added to the problems when falling and lying snow was blown into enormously high drifts and all roads in the area became blocked. The Llanelli-Kidwelly trunk road was one of the first to be closed off and the last to be opened up, as snow drifts up to 10 feet deep had effected an impenetrable obstruction near Commissioners Bridge in Kidwelly.

7

War Memorial

Kidwelly Branch War Memorial

The War Memorial dedicated to the memory of the men who gave their lives in the Great War 1914-1919 was unveiled on Saturday, July 26th, 1924, at 5 p.m. In the presence of a large gathering, on a lovely evening, the moving ceremony took place on a site, which was the gift of Dr and Miss Griffiths, Henblas, adjoining the main thoroughfare, New Street.

The memorial which was designed by Mr Glendinning Moxham, F.R.I.B.A., Swansea, is well constructed of Portland, on which stands a lifesize figure of a soldier with arms reversed. A laurel wreath has been engraved on the front of the memorial, surrounding it being the words "Gwell angau na chwilydd" and the names of 42 local boys who fell:

William James Anthony	Mervyn Jones
William C. Bowry	Oliver Jones
David Morris Davies	Samuel Jones
Frank Davies	Tudor Jones
W. Evan Davies	William Lewis
W. Stanley Davies	William Henry Lewis
David Edmunds	Wyndham Lewis
Owen L. Edwards	William John Lowe
Ivor Emanuel	Thomas Miles
Idris Evans	David John Morgan
Oliver Evans	Morgan Morgan
Alexander Gilasbey	William John Morgan
David Gower	Joseph Parry
David John Howells	George Roberts
Augustus Hugh	Stephen Sullivan
David Hughes	Freddie Stephens
Samuel Hughes	Frederick Stokes
William Hughes	Archie Styles

William James   John Tucker
Sidney M. Jenkins   Ernest Wild
Andrew Mansel   Norman H. Williams

A procession representative of the civic and social of the ancient borough was formed at the Town Hall, headed by the Police, Mynydd-y-Garreg Silver Band, Guard of Honour (which was furnished by a contingent of the 4th Batt. Welch Regt.) Ex-servicemen, Ambulance men, members of the Memorial Committee, Clergy and Ministers, Mayor and Corporation and a large number of the general public. The procession marched through Bridge Street to the memorial site, where a large gathering awaited them with all the schoolchildren in an allotted area very near the memorial.

The ceremony was opened by the singing of the Welsh hymn "Mor ddedwydd yw y rhai trwy ffydd." The Mayor (Ald. S. H. Anthony)

Borough of Kidwelly.

▸◂

PROGRAMME

OF THE

Unveiling Ceremony

OF THE

Kidwelly Borough War Memorial

To the Memory of our Men who gave their
lives in the Great War, 1914—1919.

Saturday, July 26th, 1924, at 5 p.m.

"Mercury" Offices, 28, Market Street, Llanelly.

(Courtesy Mrs Margaret Hughes).

In Loving Memory

OF

Private Archie Styles,

(14th Welsh Regiment),

Son of CHARLES and EMILY STYLES, Old Shop,
Kidwelly,

Who fell in action in France on May 4th, 1918.

AGED 21 YEARS.

We do not know what pain he bore,
We never saw him die ;
We only know he passed away,
And never said, " Good-bye."

(Courtesy Mrs Margaret Hughes).

In Affectionate Remembrance of

Pte. William Henery Lewis,

Beloved son of Edwin and Fanny Lewis,

Killed in action on April 20th, 1916,

Aged 22 years.

We lttle thought when he left home
He would no more return,
That he so soon in death would sleep
So far away from home.

(Courtesy Mr Arthur Lewis).

presided, supported by the Deputy Mayor (Dr Griffiths), the Town Clerk (Mr W. R. James), and the members of the Council and Memorial Committee. Amongst those present were: Sir Alfred and Lady Stephens (Broomhill), Sir Alfred and Lady Mond, Lieut. Col. W. N. Jones (High Sheriff), Major John Francis, D.S.O., Carmarthen, Chief Constable of Carmarthen, Mr W. Picton Phillips, Mr and Mrs H. E. Smart (Mountain View) and Capt. H. Glyn Edwards (Welsh Area British Legion), Rev. R. Curzon Jones, Rev. E. J. Herbert, Rev. H. R. Jones, Rev. Ambrose Jones, M.A., Rev. D. A. Morgan, Rev. Curig Davies.

When prayers had been offered and hymn singing was over, Capt. D. Brynmor Anthony, MA, MC (Registrar of the University of Wales), one of the most distinguished local men in the Great War, read out the Roll of Honour. Captain Anthony, a native of Kidwelly, had achieved a distinguished career in the army, rising from the rank of private in the Royal Welsh Fusiliers to become captain, and gaining the Military Cross with Bar, as well as the Silver Medal of the Italian Government. Captain Anthony read out the tribute as inscribed on the monument, and observed they should carry out the spirit of the sacrifice and willingness to stand for principles of righteousness against evil which had charac-terised the men who answered duty's call from 1914 to 1919.

Military Cross (George V issue). (Photograph: Author).

Unveiling of the monument was then undertaken by Mrs Margaret Hughes of Gwendraeth Terrace – this part of the ceremony in par-ticular creating an aura of emotion and sensitivity, Mrs Hughes having lost three of her sons in the conflict for freedom. The memorial was dedicated by the Rev. D. Ambrose Jones, MA, after which a one minute silence was observed. Sir Alfred Stephens, JP, CC, said that as a fellow townsman he felt proud to take part in the unveiling of the memorial. He recalled with pride the spirit and determination of the local lads, who were amongst the first to fight the country's battles, also that the relatives of those brave heroes could have con-solation in the fact that their names would live forever. Ex-Alderman Thomas Reynolds, as Chairman of the First War Memorial Committee, said he felt proud at having been present at such a magnificent

Mrs Margaret Hughes, who lost three sons
in the Great War, 1914-1919.
(Photograph courtesy Mrs Jennifer Denman).

gathering. Major John Francis said that some of the men whose names were inscribed on the monument had served under him in the East. They had been the first to volunteer and that this occasion must be a joy to all ex-servicemen to know that their comrades were not forgotten. Lieut Col. W. N. Jones complimented the people upon the handsome monument they had erected. Had it not been for their sacrifice the chapels and churches, castles and homes would have been demolished as they had been in France and Belgium. Sir Alfred Mond, Bart, said he felt highly honoured in being asked to participate in the ceremony. There were few families in the country whose homes had not been visited by the Angel of Death, and there were few hearths which did not have an empty chair, and he hoped that never again would the world be plunged into the horrors of a similar war.

E. J. Gower (Secretary of the Memorial Committee) in handing over the Memorial to the Mayor and Corporation, said that he: ". . . deemed it the greatest honour of his life to carry out such a glorious duty. He felt extremely proud of his part in having helped to erect such a magnificent memorial to the beloved fallen. Their names would stand immortal and for future ages the memorial would testify to their great sacrifice. Whatever his humble efforts had been, they vanished away in the light of the glorious and great sacrifice of his beloved comrades on the field of battle!" Mr Gower thanked all members of the Committee for all their hard work, especially treasurer Cllr. David Davies. The Mayor (Ald. S. H. Anthony) in accepting the memorial expressed thanks to all involved, also to Mr John Thomas (Velindre) who headed the subscriptions with a hundred guineas, and Dr Griffiths and Miss May Griffiths for donating the site. Cllr. Dr. T. R. Griffiths formally handed over the site to the Borough Council.

Wreaths were then placed around the memorial by Ex-Servicemen, the Band of Hope, the War Memorial Committee, the Borough Council, relatives and friends, with the British Legion wreath being placed in the centre.

Mynydd-y-Garreg Silver Band played the 'Dead March', after which the Rev. E. J. Herbert pronounced the Benediction. Sounding of the 'Last Post' and 'Reveille' by Sgt. T. Loverbridge of Swansea and a massed choir conducted by Mr Francis Reynolds singing 'Hen Wlad Fy Nhadau' and 'God Save the King', terminated a most impressive ceremony.

The gathering then adjourned to an informal meeting of the Town Council held at the site, at which the 'Freedom of the Borough' was conferred on the following citizens by virtue of having achieved distinction in the war:

> Capt. D. Brynmor Anthony, M.C. with Bar and Italian Medal.
> Sgt. Sidney Rees, D.C.M.
> Lance-Corpl. D. C. Gibbard, D.C.M.
> Private T. R. Wild, D.C.M.
> Corpl. D. W. Williams, M.M. and Bar
> Lance-Corpl. Joseph Emanuel, M.M.
> Lance Corpl. Evan H. Rees, M.M.
> Lance-Corpl. E. D. Williams, M.M.
> Guardsman W. J. Thomas, M.M.
> Private Vernon Wilkins, M.M.
> Sgt. Idris Evans, M.M. (deceased)

and Mrs Ida Jane Richards who was awarded the Medal of the Order of the British Empire for gallantry at Pembrey Munition Works. The

War Memorial, 2003.
(Photograph: Author).

ceremony was performed by the Mayor (Ald. S. H. Anthony) and Town Clerk (Mr. W. R. James).

This was a special day in the history of the Ancient Borough, with the handsome memorial a tribute to those brave heroes who gave their lives in the First World War and I feel proud to record such a moving ceremony.

8

Kidwelly Murder Trial

DIARY OF EVENTS

1881

Wednesday, February 2nd	John Thomas, 11 years old, missing.
Thursday, February 3rd	Search parties organised.
Friday, February 4th	Young boy's body discovered.
Friday, February 4th	Two brothers arrested.
Friday, February 4th	Mother of the brothers arrested later.
Saturday, February 5th	Inquest at Guildhall, Kidwelly.
Monday, February 7th	Magisterial Enquiry, Kidwelly.
Monday, February 7th	Funeral at Llansaint.
Friday, February 11th	Magisterial Enquiry resumed.
Thursday, May 12th	Murder trial at Guildhall in Swansea.

A LIST OF PEOPLE INVOLVED IN THE CASE

Master John Thomas, 11 years old	Deceased boy.
Mr Evan Thomas, Shoemaker	Father.
Mrs Letitia Thomas, Housewife	Mother.
Mrs Jane Mazey, Dressmaker Master David Mazey, 12 years Master Benjamin Mazey, 10 years	All accused of murder.
Mr David Mazey, Shingler	Husband and father of accused boys.
Mr David Thomas, Tin Worker	Discovered the deceased boy.
Miss Margaret Anthony, Housekeeper	Muddlescombe Farm.
Mrs Ann Hughes, Housewife	Stockwell Bank.
Mr David Hughes, Blacksmith	Stockwell Bank.
Mrs Lily Walters, Servant	Stockwell Bank.

Mrs Rhoda Evans, Housewife	Penybanc, Stockwell.
Police Sergeant John Jones	Kidwelly.
Police Constable John Williams	Pembrey.
Police Constable William Thomas	Pembrey.
Police Constable William James	Ferryside.
Dr David Jones, Coroner and Medical Practitioner	Kidwelly.
Dr J. Arthur Jones, Medical Practitioner	Llanelly.
Dr William Morgan, County Analyst	Swansea.
Mr John Jones, Lock-up Keeper	Town hall, Kidwelly.
Mr William Jones, Shopkeeper	Kidwelly.
Mrs Margaret White, Shopkeeper	Kidwelly.
Mrs Simms, Housewife	Kidwelly.
Mrs Frances Gower, Housewife	Stockwell Lane.
Mrs Mary Morgan, Housewife	Penybont, Stockwell.
Superintendent Harries	Llanelly Police.
Chief Constable Capt. Phillips	Llanelly Police.
Cllr. David Harries	Mayor of Kidwelly.
Mr Mansel Rees	Deputy Recorder Kidwelly.
Mr. T. W. A. Evans	Former Mayor of Kidwelly.
Mr Richard Williams	Surveyor, Burry Port.
Rev. William Sinnett	Vicar of Kidwelly.
Mr George Spurrell	Magistrate's Clerk, Carmarthen.
Mr T. B. Snead, Llanelly	Prosecuting Solicitor at the Magisterial Enquiry.
Mr William Howell, Llanelly	Defending Solicitor at the Magisterial Enquiry.
Mr Justice Flave	Presiding Judge at the trial.
Mr Bowen, Q.C., and Mr Abel Thomas	Prosecuting Counsel and assistant at the trial.
Mr Bowen Rowlands	Defence Counsel at the trial.
Mr C. Fowler	Jury Foreman at the trial.

KIDWELLY MURDER TRIAL

A mother and her two sons in custody
Almost unparalleled for being horrific and brutal and also due to
the inoffensive nature of the victim, is the tragic event that occurred
in Kidwelly on February 2nd, 1881. A young boy's alleged murder

took place in broad daylight in the quiet little town of Kidwelly, a town renowned for its tranquillity and absence of sensational crimes. As a result of this heinous act, the whole town was stunned, indeed the whole county was affected, and the murder was the main topic of conversation throughout the area. Details of the murder though, were so enshrouded in mystery, the general public jumped to the conclusion that those taken into custody were the culprits. Such a concept led to a chain of bitter repugnant reactions against the accused.

Victim of the atrocious crime was John Thomas, a young lad, age 11, son of Evan Thomas, Shoemaker, who lived with his family – wife and eight children – in Chapel House, Tin Mill Row. The mother

Mrs Hannah Evans (Thomas), centre, sister of the deceased,
with her family – son Brynmor and daughters
Kathleen and Jessie.
(Photograph courtesy Brynmor Evans).

and father were natives of Llansaint but since their marriage had set up home in Kidwelly. Their eldest child, a girl, was employed at the Kidwelly Tinplate Works. The family lived in adverse circumstances and there was great compassion for them.

Charged with the murder were Jane Mazey and her two sons – David and Benjamin – wife and sons of David Mazey, Shingler at Kidwelly Tinplate Works. David Mazey was an Irishman and prisoner Jane Mazey was a native of Cilgerran, a village in Pembrokeshire. She was David Mazey's second wife and the two children in custody with her were their natural progeny. She had four other children, the eldest being employed by the same firm as his father and the three younger children were at home. Neighbours described Mrs Mazey as being a very aggressive and vindictive woman. Quarrels in the family were said to be frequent but David Mazey was generally regarded as being inoffensive.

The two accused children were said to be very mischievous, having had too much of their own way with their mother, who paradoxically, was sometimes violent toward them. Discourse in the community recalled one dubious incident in particular, when in the previous August the boys were implicated in a questionable accident. It seems that the boys now in custody, in company with another boy by the name of Fisher aged nine years, made their way to an embankment. In a matter of only about 30 minutes later the two Mazey boys returned, carrying the clothes of their companion and saying he had drowned. At an inquest on that event, the boy David appeared as a witness. He said that Fisher walked into the water to bathe and sank out of sight at once. The whole town was agog with rumours re-garding statements made by the boys 'outside' and the affair at that time was deemed to be suspect.

EVENTS LEADING UP TO THE ALLEGED MURDER

On Wednesday, 2nd February, 1881, John Thomas, the young boy later found deceased, was sent by his father on an errand to a Mr Anthony of Muddlescombe Farm situated on the outskirts of Kidwelly. A few minutes after 1 o'clock he set off to deliver a pair of shoes for which he was to be paid nine shillings. He arrived at the farm safely, was given dinner and left at about half past 2 o'clock with a half-sovereign given by Miss Anthony on the understanding that he would bring back the change of one shilling. The home of the deceased boy and

Muddlescombe Farm were about a mile distance apart, and between, was a house called 'Stockwell', home of David Mazey and his family. On his way back home, John was seen by a Mrs Ann Hughes, who lived across the road, being accosted by David Mazey (one of the boys in custody). He came into view from another direction, carrying some cans, having delivered dinner to his father. The Mazey boy asked John to come into the house and when John stopped by the entrance gate, David was heard to say that his mother was not in. Both were seen entering the house and the door was closed by David Mazey. John was not seen alive again.

A short time after the boys had gone in, Jane Mazey was seen as she returned from the village, going into the house. Later on in the day, John's family became anxious when he did not return, and were even more so as the absence prolonged. They made enquiries but failed to find out anything about his whereabouts. On being told that he was in the habit of playing with the Mazey boys, John's mother called at their house. Jane Mazey came to the door and denied that John had been there, but refused to ask her boys about the missing John, saying they were in bed asleep. During the night there was a thorough search of all places where it was imagined John might be found, but there was no sign of him anywhere.

On the Thursday morning, John's father called at the home of Mrs Ann Hughes, who told him to ask at Mazey's house, as she had seen John going in there. He replied that his wife had already been in Stockwell House on the previous evening and had been told that John had not been there.

On the Thursday night, Jane Mazey called at the Thomas' home, and asked if the boy had been found. On being told 'no', she asked whether they had searched the haystacks, indirectly suggesting that John could be hiding. She was told that they had searched everywhere they thought he might possibly be. Amazingly, then Jane Mazey stated that John had been playing on her hearthstone, with a

half-sovereign wrapped in brown paper. She added that he had given half-a-crown to one of her boys, and that they should not worry about the money as she would give them a half-sovereign on payday, which was the following Saturday. John's mother replied it was not the money she wanted, it was her boy she wanted.

Half-sovereign.

Prior to Jane Mazey's visit, John's parents surmised that maybe he had lost the money and was now hiding. Jane's remarks though changed this trend of thought, which gave a new and different slant on their conjectures. Seeds of suspicion took hold.

A BODY IS FOUND

The search continued next morning and one of the searchers by the name of David Thomas came across a piece of cloth just visible above the weeds and grass near a hedge in Mazey's garden. He bent down to scrape away the loose grass, found the boy's body, then ran quickly to fetch the police, who were in Mazey's house at the time. He shouted: 'I've found the body'. P.S. John Jones made his way to the garden and saw the body lying face down. Turning him over, he saw that the skull was completely split open. He took the two boys into custody and when more information came to light, the mother was also arrested and taken into custody. On Friday all three were brought before the magistrates and formally charged with wilful murder.

When news broke that John's body had been found, public emotions rose to fever pitch throughout the town and neighbourhood. The deplorable manner of the crime in such a quiet rural area was to cause a frenzy of reaction in the community.

People gathered at a spot opposite the police station house, anxious to catch a glimpse of the accused. News spread rapidly to neighbouring towns and villages and regular routine railway trains brought more strangers and spectators into the ancient borough. On Friday, a decision was made to hold an inquest on Saturday morning.

SCENE OF THE ALLEGED MURDER

A large number of people had gathered at 'Stockwell', scene of the evil crime. The house was of old-fashioned construction and in the past was deemed to be one of the finest houses in Kidwelly, yet was now in a rather dilapidated state.

There was a large lawn at the front of the house surrounded by walls, and running alongside these walls were ten trees, six on one side and four on the other. Several windows were without panes of glass and articles of clothing were draped over them – sure evidence of poverty. Parallel with the house were ruins of former buildings –

now broken-down walls. At the back of the house there was an extensive garden, about 70 yards long and 35 yards wide. A small outhouse occupied one part and from this building ran a small drain about two feet in depth. The drain had been neglected and the sides had fallen in, filling the culvert to a depth where it was almost level with the surface of the garden. Rubbish such as weeds had also been thrown into the culvert causing it to be barely visible. It was in this culvert that John Thomas's weed-covered body was discovered.

A makeshift swing dangled from an apple tree in the middle of the plot. The tree was of slender proportions and the swing was made of rope with a stick attached to it. The Mazeys invented a story and claimed that while John was swinging there he had struck the tree with such force as to cause fatal injuries to his face and head. The two young brothers were so frightened by the incident they decided to hide the body. However, this theory was discounted by medical evidence, besides which there was not a trace of blood anywhere near the tree and the boy had lost a vast amount of blood.

Kidwelly town Hall .1905.

PB03

INQUEST ON THE BODY

On Saturday, February 5th, an inquest on John Thomas's body was held at the Guildhall, Kidwelly. Present were the Coroner, Cllr. David Harries, Mayor, Gwenllian House, and the Deputy Recorder Mr Mansel Rees. Mr T. W. A. Evans, a former Mayor of the town, served as Foreman of the Jury, and jury members were James Williams, Thomas Griffiths, John Morgan, Thomas Anthony, John Wild, Richard Morgan, Evan Williams, John Gower, Francis Randell, William Randell, Thomas Morgan and Joseph Wild. Superintendent Harries of Llanelly represented the police authorities. The accused trio were not present. Post-mortem examination was carried out by Dr David Jones of Kidwelly and Dr J. Arthur Jones, Llanelly, prior to commencement of the inquest which was due to start at 12 noon. The jury were sworn in and were then required to view the lad's body.

The first witness to be called was the deceased boy's father, Evan Thomas, Shoemaker of Chapel House, Tin Mill Row, Kidwelly. He stated – "I last saw my son John, 11 years of age, on Wednesday, February 2nd, at about fifteen minutes past one, when I sent him to Muddlescombe Farm with a pair of shoes. I did not see him alive again."

Another witness, Margaret Anthony said – "I am the daughter of Thomas Anthony of Muddlescombe Farm and act as housekeeper. I knew John Thomas, the deceased, he came to the farm with a pair of boots for me. I gave him half-a-sovereign in payment for the boots, I also gave him some dinner. I wrapped up the half-sovereign in a piece of brown paper and he left at about half past two o'clock."

Ann Hughes, wife of David Hughes, who lived across the road opposite the Mazey's House at Stockwell Bank, said – "I knew John Thomas well. On Wednesday afternoon last between half past three and four o'clock, I saw him by the entrance gate of Stockwell House, residence of David Mazey. Mazey's little boy David was with him. I saw them both going into the house, the boy Mazey slamming the door after them. I did not see anyone playing with them.

"On the following morning at about ten o'clock, Evan Thomas, father of the deceased, called on me; I then told him I had seen his boy going into the Mazey's house on the previous day. That afternoon I had a conversation with Jane Mazey. It commenced between my servant Lily Walters, who asked her where the boy had gone from her house the previous evening. I heard Jane Mazey deny that John Thomas had been at her home the previous day. Hearing this, I went out into the road and said – 'Yes he was at your house, I saw him going in'. She answered, 'Don't you tell lies'. I replied, 'It was not a lie and I swear I saw him going in'. She said I was a liar and that he had not been at her house the previous day."

Dr David Jones stated – "I am a surgeon practising at Kidwelly. I carried out a post-mortem examination of the deceased this morning. Dr J. A. Jones was also present. After taking off the clothes which were damp, I noticed that the body was covered with marks and a greenish hue, showing signs that decomposition had set in. On the right shoulder, near the lower part of the shoulder blade, there was a bruise. The skull had been opened from the right eye, across the bridge of the nose, through to the left eye. All the bones of the skull cap were broken to pieces, all the brain had disappeared, except a part of the small brain which was loose and had evidently been put back. The upper jaw was smashed and the lower part broken in four places caused apparently by some blunt instrument. The injuries inflicted upon the head were something terrible. On opening the chest and belly, I saw the main organs quite healthy but nearly devoid of blood."

The Coroner stated – "I do not think it possible that the fracture of the skull could have been caused by a fall, the state of the body rendered that to me not possible. It is possible, but I do not think it probable that two boys of 10 and 12 years old could have caused the injuries, I cannot help the jury as to what caused them, but I believe it was a blunt instrument, It might have been a hammer. I found in the stomach some undigested food. I believe he was murdered before five o'clock Wednesday afternoon. The food he had at Muddlescombe Farm would not have had time to be digested in that time. I believe therefore he was murdered within three hours after he partook of his dinner on that Wednesday."

Dr James Arthur Jones said – "I am a medical practitioner and reside at Llanelly. I attended Dr David Jones on his post-mortem examination of the deceased, and assisted him. I have just heard his evidence and I fully agree with it. There is nothing I can add to it."

David Hughes said – "I live at Stockwell Bank and am a blacksmith. On Wednesday last, between three and four o'clock, I saw Jane Mazey coming from the direction of the town, and entering the house. I did not see her leave the house afterwards."

Lily Walters stated – "I am a servant in the service of the last witness. On Wednesday last, I was feeding the fowls opposite our door, when Jane Mazey who was putting out clothes, asked if I heard whether the boy had been found or not. I said I did not think so, and she said, 'it seems as if the earth has swallowed him up'. I then asked her where did he go from your house? She said – 'My house! He has not been in my house'. I answered yes he has, for Mrs Hughes saw him go in."

In his statement David Thomas said – "I am a labourer and live at Tin Mill Row. I was one, amongst others, that was searching for the body. I was on top of a hedge, I and a man named Frederick Lloyd, looking down at David Mazey's garden, when we saw a piece of cloth, which afterwards proved to be the trousers of the deceased, in a ditch or drain, with a lot of weeds over it. I jumped off the hedge, and in order to make sure that it was the body, drew some of them off. I knew John Thomas, the deceased, and ran at once to fetch the police, through Mazey's back door, shouting that I had found the dead body in Mazey's garden. Jane Mazey was then coming up from the kitchen, and hearing my cry, she started crying – 'Oh my dear Benjamin, poor little fellow'. With this Police Sergeant John Jones came down from the upstairs of Mazey's house and together we went out to the garden."

Letitia Thomas, mother of the unfortunate boy, was next to give evidence. She was unable to walk without assistance and in words mingled with sobs said – "I was at Mazey's house on Wednesday night and knocked at the door. Jane Mazey came to the door, it was then between seven and eight o'clock. I asked her if she'd seen my boy. She answered – 'Not today'. I then asked her if one of her sons had seen him. She said, no David her son was ill in bed since four o'clock and that she had bundled Benjamin after him, and that both were then sleeping. Her husband told her to see as to the children but she did not do so. She stated before I left that I could make my mind easy, my child would probably return before morning."

David Mazey, father of the boys, husband of the woman in custody said – "I am a shingler at Kidwelly Tinworks, and live at Stockwell House. I returned from work on Wednesday evening last at 7.30. I knew nothing of the death of the deceased but what I have heard. I cannot account for the body being found in my garden. My children were in bed when I came home on Wednesday. They slept in the same room as myself. I remember the mother of the deceased coming to my house in the evening. When I heard my wife saying she intended going to Muddlescombe to look for the deceased, I told her there was no need for her to do so, as probably the boy was playing some-where. I did not notice anything strange about the house."

Police Sergeant John Jones stated – "The body was entirely covered, with the exception of a small part of the trousers on the hip. I turned the body over and a portion of the brain fell out, and I saw that the skull was broken. I put the brain back in the skull. The body of the deceased was conveyed home. After finding the body in the garden, I apprehended the two boys and afterwards the woman."

The jury retired and returned in about ten minutes with a verdict that: "John Thomas came to his death by injuries inflicted on his skull by some blunt instrument, having been wilfully murdered by a person of persons unknown."

THE MAGISTERIAL ENQUIRY

The public awaited anxiously for this Enquiry as it was generally believed the result would largely dispel the mystery in which the whole case was enshrouded. The Enquiry was held on Monday, 7th February, but as the 'ordinary' monthly sessions fell on that day, the case did not commence until nearly four o'clock in the afternoon. Nevertheless, the Town Hall was crowded to full capacity all day.

After the 'ordinary' cases had been dispensed, and an adjournment of half an hour declared, the hall was cleared. When this had been done, the prisoners were brought up from the cells below. Within a few minutes of the vacation, the locked hall door was besieged by a throng who tried to burst it open. The magistrate's officials were forced to use a private entrance at the back of the building to gain access. When all was considered to be ready, the hall door was opened and there was a desperate rush to find places – the room was full to bursting point in a matter of minutes.

The presiding magistrate, Cllr. Harries, extended a welcome to all so long as they kept quiet. He said the proceedings could be lawfully suspended if the spectators were not quiet and orderly. Later on, he threatened to clear the court on two or three occasions as the onlookers would not maintain silence.

Sight of the three prisoners engendered feelings of remorse and pity. Remorse that because in this civilisation (of which we boast) it was possible for a seven-months pregnant mother to be placed in such a position and be charged with such a horrendous crime. Pity because of the dire position in which she and her children, age ten and twelve, found themselves. It was a sad spectacle indeed. Jane

Mazey was a very tall, strongly built woman, of sallow complexion, her demeanour sullen and morose. She sat on a chair opposite the bench, the younger of the two boys on her right, the elder to the right of his brother. The mother and the elder boy never looked up, except when something striking caught their attention, and then only momentarily, e.g. when the charge was read out.

The husband and father, in court during the hearing appeared to be quite overcome by the whole procedure. He wept bitterly and his eyes were fixed on the trio; their eyes though, did not meet his. The scene was totally heart-rending.

The officiating magistrates were Cllr. D. Harries (Mayor), T. W. A. Evans (ex-Mayor) and Mr Mansel Rees, (Deputy Recorder). The police authorities were represented by Chief Constable Capt. Phillips and Superintendent Harries of Llanelly, and Mr George Spurrell of Carmarthen served as Clerk. Mr T. B. Snead, Solicitor, Llanelly, appeared for the prosecution and Mr William Howell, Llanelly, for the defence. The evidence generally was the same as that given at the inquest and Mr Snead stated he would examine only one or two witnesses. On behalf of the prosecution representative he would then ask for a remand so that the police could have time to gather evidence.

The first witness was Evan Thomas, the father, who said – "I sent my boy with boots to Muddlescombe Farm for which he was to be paid nine shillings. Before he left home he had his dinner."

The accused was asked if she had any questions to ask the witness. Standing up and with great difficulty at first, she spoke in Welsh and asked "Do you think I did it?"

He replied – "I think it was done between you" (meaning her and the two children).

Margaret Anthony of Muddlescombe Farm said that on the previous Wednesday she gave the deceased half-a-sovereign for the boots brought by him. The boots were to the value of nine shillings but she had no change, so she gave him half-a-sovereign on the understanding he was to bring one shilling back. He left the farm at about 2.30 p.m., she believed for home and he was quite well. He did not bring back the change.

Ann Hughes, wife of David Hughes, blacksmith, Stockwell Bank, said she did not see either of the children coming out again after they went into the Mazey House.

Jane Mazey then asked the witness – "Did I use the words 'That it seems as if the earth had swallowed him up?'"

Witness replied – "Yes, I heard you say so to my servant Lily Walters."

The prisoner stated forcibly – "I did not say it."

Lily Walters, the servant referred to, corroborated the evidence of the last witness, and stated Jane Mazey had used the words.

David Hughes, a blacksmith who lived across the road opposite the prisoners' home, said he: ". . . saw Jane Mazey coming from town between three and four o'clock in the afternoon on Wednesday last."

Dr David Jones in his statement said he: ". . . believed the murder was committed within three hours from the time the boy had his dinner."

Arrangements had been made for a vehicle to be standing by outside the hall to take the prisoners to the railway station when the enquiry was over. When the detainees appeared and were ushered into the waiting trap, there were no disturbances from the waiting crowd, but taunts and boos could be heard distinctly when the discredited family passed an angry group hanging around the Pelican Hotel. At the station, police constables accompanied the three prisoners as they boarded the train for a journey to Carmarthen gaol and detention there.

Pelican Hotel, Kidwelly 1884.

As it was not common knowledge that the prisoners would be leaving Kidwelly, only a few showed up at the railway station and there were no public demonstrations. The station was located quite some distance away from the town.

Clothes belonging to the prisoners were sent to the County Analyst for examination, and his report was expected to be in the hands of the magistrates on the following Friday.

FUNERAL OF THE BOY

Monday, February 7th

Both parents of the murdered lad were natives of Llansaint and so their son's funeral took place at All Saints Church followed by inter-

All Saints Church - Llansaint. PBQ3.

ment in the churchyard. A large number of people attended and without doubt the number would have been trebled had there not been a downpour of rain at the time; also, the ongoing enquiry coincided with the event. Neither the mother nor the father were able to attend the funeral to pay their last respects; nevertheless, there was a large family gathering. The bereaved parents were vital witnesses compelled to be present at the enquiry, the mother being the first witness on the stand that very morning. Rev. William Sinnett, Vicar of Kidwelly, officiated at the graveside.

MAGISTERIAL ENQUIRY RESUMES

Monday, February 7th

Mrs Letitia Thomas, mother of the deceased boy, on stating what had taken place at the Mazey's house, was asked if she had seen Jane Mazey anywhere else around that time.

She replied – "Oh yes, on Thursday, the following day, she called at my house and said she had seen my boy on the hearthstone with a half-sovereign in brown paper and that he had gone out of her house to change it, returned and gave half a crown to her son Benjamin. 'He had then', she said 'gone home'. She also told me not to mind about the money as she would return the half-sovereign on the following Saturday. Rhoda Evans was present at this conversation. I do not remember any more."

Cross-examined by Mr Howell, she was asked why there was no mention of the visit to her house by Jane Mazey at the Coroner's inquest. She replied – "I gave my evidence as far as I was questioned. I knew I was sworn to say all I had to say on the matter, and as far as I was examined I did so. I did not say one word of the second statement I have made today as I was not asked as to what took place at my house. I did not understand when I was before the Coroner that I was to say everything I knew, but I understood I was to answer all I was asked."

Rhoda Evans, wife of William Evans, Doubler, of Penybank, Stockwell, was the next to give evidence. She confirmed she was at the house of Evan Thomas at the time of Jane Mazey's alleged visit and she endorsed the evidence of Letitia Thomas regarding the conversation which had taken place on that day and at that time.

David Thomas then described how he had found the body.

Mary Morgan, wife of Daniel Morgan, Engineer at Messrs Redford's Brickyard, Kidwelly, residing at Penybont, Stockwell, said – "On Thursday morning, between eight and nine o'clock on the 3rd of this month, Jane Mazey came to my house for the loan of a tub of mine, which she wanted for washing. I lent her the tub, she took it with her. I heard at seven o'clock the previous evening that John Thomas was missing. There is but a small distance from our house to the Mazeys. On Thursday evening, hearing that he was still missing, I went to Jane Mazey's house and asked whether she had seen the boy playing with her children. She said 'I have not seen him'. This took place about six o'clock. I know the two boys in

Remains of Redford's Brickyard, near Brickyard Cottages, 2003.
(Photograph: Author).

custody and on the occasion of my visit, I saw the eldest of the two –
David – washing the hearthstone. He was on his knees. I cannot say
whether there was anything out of the way on the hearthstone, I did
not notice it!"

Cross-examined by Mr Howell she stated – "I did not notice
anything peculiar about the hearthstone. He was stoning – chalking
it when I left. I do not think it unusual to chalk the hearthstone, nor
do I see anything remarkable in washing it. I did not take much notice
of it, and so cannot say whether there was anything particular about
the hearthstone."

The Mayor intervened here – "It was a large room and I could not
have seen blood on the hearthstone, even if it was there. It is customary
for children to wash the hearthstone. I have seen them do it many
times."

The next witness, William Jones, Shopkeeper, Bridge Street said – "I know the youngest prisoner, Benjamin Mazey. On Thursday morning, February 3rd, he came to my shop. I did not see anyone with him. He asked me to change half-a-sovereign for him. He did not show it to me and so I did not see it. I did not change it for him."

Cross-examined by Mr Howell, he stated: "It was a very common thing for people to come to my shop to ask for change. There is no bank here and they generally go where change can be had. A good many boys were in the habit of coming into the shop. I had money when Benjamin Mazey called, but I did not change it for him as my wife was at the time ill in bed, and I was in a hurry, so I had no time." At this point T. W. A. Evans again intervened stating – "The examination on this question is not of any importance and it is a simple waste of the bench time."

Mr Howell retorted – "Of course, if your minds are already made up."

Mr Evans replied – "Oh, no, not at all."

Mr Howell continued – "I submit that the case is a very important one, the charge being that of murder, and I think that some latitude should be given to me in my cross-examination of witnesses. Besides, I think I have treated the bench very fairly, for I have not occupied the bench more than five minutes in cross-examining any one witness. I think I have sufficient knowledge of my profession not to put any question without having a definite objective in view."

Mr Evans intimated that he had intended no imputation on Mr Howell and the matter was dropped.

The last witness re-examined by Mr Snead – "I have no doubt whatever but that the boy who asked me to change the half-sovereign was the prisoner Benjamin Mazey."

The most damning evidence against the boys was the certain knowledge that on the day following the murder, both had called at a certain shop to ask for change of half-a-sovereign but their request was rejected. They tried again at the next door shop and this time the coin was changed without hindrance. Three shillings and seven-pence halfpenny of this had been spent and the remaining six shillings and fourpence halfpenny was found in their possession when they were arrested.

Police Sgt. John Jones took the stand and stated – "I am a police sergeant stationed at Kidwelly. On Thursday, February 3rd, I was informed that John Thomas, the deceased, was missing since the previous evening. In consequence of this and other information, I went first to the deceased's father's house and together with the father I proceeded to the Mazey's house for the purpose of making enquiries as to the missing boy. On arriving at the house I told Jane Mazey that I wanted to see two of her boys, David and Benjamin, in order to make enquiries of them as to John Thomas' disappearance. She told me they were in bed and she would accompany me upstairs. Myself, Evan Thomas and Jane Mazey then went upstairs. I enquired of the boys about John Thomas. David Mazey said he had seen him the previous afternoon, when he had been there, they had been playing together on the swing in the garden, and that the deceased had shown them half-a-sovereign, after which he had again wrapped it in brown paper, put it in his pocket and that he had gone home from the garden through the back lane by Stockwell Road. During the whole time

Stockwell Lane, 2003.
(Photograph: Author).

David told me this, Benjamin cried bitterly. On asking them about the money they had been spending in the town, both at first denied it but afterwards David said he borrowed a shilling on his mother's name from Mrs Simms. Benjamin contradicted David and said it was half-a-crown they had borrowed. Jane Mazey here went out of the house saying she was going to Mrs Simms to ask whether they had the money there. At 6 o'clock the same evening I searched the house thinking that perhaps John Thomas might be hiding there somewhere. We went to an old well at the back of the house, which we found filled then to the centre of the garden, to the swing upon which the boys said they had been swinging but found nothing. We then left the house. On returning we met in Lady Street Jane Mazey. She told me the boys had no money off Mrs Simms and that she was going home to get out of her boys where they had the money. As soon, she added, as she would find out she would let me know. About forty minutes after, she called at my house and said the two boys admitted having half-a-crown from John Thomas. She also told me that she was going to the missing boy's home to tell his mother the same thing. On Friday morning, 4th February, I again went to Stockwell House and downstairs I saw Jane Mazey and David. I asked where Benjamin was and on being told that he was upstairs I went up and found him. I had a conversation with him about the half-sovereign, in the course of which he told me that failing to have it changed at Wm. Jones (the last witness), he had gone next door and had it changed with Margaret White, Shopkeeper, Bridge Street. It was not him he said who had stolen it but David his brother. John Thomas placed the half-a-sovereign, he said, in some loose paper on the table, his brother David took it and gave it to him to go and get it changed. Afterwards they divided it equally between them. He added he had spent some of the money but that the remainder was hid under a gate and that the remainder of his brother's money was hid under another gate lower down the road. Going out to the places he told me of, I found under some stones by a gate leading to the house, in a box, two shillings and a threepenny piece, and one shilling and sixpence halfpenny in coppers, beside a box of fuses. At the other gate, going 100 yards from the house, I found two shillings in silver, and ninepence halfpenny in coppers. They were concealed on the top of the hedge. The boy further said that the last sight he had of the deceased was his going through Stockwell gate, going in the direction of Trimsaran. At this point I was called by the witness David Thomas, who said that the little boy's body had been found. Mrs

Mazey and the boys burst out crying and she said 'Oh dear Benjamin', two or three times. I then arrested both boys, on a charge of murdering John Thomas. About ten yards from where the body was found, I found a tobacco pipe and stem, which Evan Thomas identified as belonging to his son. I also found a garden spade (produced as evidence) with dirt and grass on it, and in the house a pincers, a smoothing iron, a hammer and a mattock. There were a few hairs on the mattock and some dust on the smoothing iron.

On Tuesday last I found some brains in the garden of Mrs Frances Gower, which is separated by land from the Mazey garden. The brain I showed to Dr Jones and he told me to place it in methylated spirits. The sergeant then produced the exhibit. I also found a quantity of clothing – some of the prisoners – on which I believe there was blood, and I sent it to the analyst. I sent a cloth jacket and corduroy trousers belonging to each of the boys, and a pair of boots and a cap of Benjamin's.

"Later that Friday morning, the 4th instant, I also charged Jane Mazey with the murder, after the arrest of the boys. She said nothing, but cried. I have a gown that Mrs Gower gave me on Monday evening, as belonging to Mrs Jane Mazey, and I have sent it to the analyst."

Cross-examined by Mr Howell, the sergeant stated – "I have been in the police force for about 20 years. I gave some evidence before the Coroner, but not all, as he told me it was not necessary, and that I could give it another time. As a police officer, I know I was sworn to tell the truth, and the whole truth, and so I did."

The Mayor stated here that at the inquest, the police sergeant was about to relate the circumstances connected with the prisoners. He stopped him and told him he only needed the evidence that showed a murder had been committed.

The cross-examination continued and the sergeant said – "The body was found at the upper part of the garden. When I came to the body, it was not all in sight. On Wednesday, the day of the disappearance, we had very showery and very wet weather, and we had heavy rain on Thursday as well. I found footmarks all over the place. There were so many marks there that I could not distinguish between them. When I went upstairs to the boys on Thursday evening, it was then about 8.30 p.m. As soon as I came into the room, I asked them about the missing boy. I did not ask them many times, only two or three times. Evan Thomas and Jane Mazey were in the room at the same time. I was 'all there' uniform and all, and they could not have made a mistake as to who I was. Benjamin seemed frightened when I came into the room and began to cry. I did not caution him before he made the statement to me. Benjamin did not contradict himself in what he told me." (Witness here became rather confused, Mr Howell referring to his statement on this point in his examination, when he had stated that both had denied that they had any money. Eventually, the witness said that he had made a mistake, if he had stated that Benjamin had denied it.)

He continued – "When I searched the house on Thursday evening I did not make a very stringent search, as we were simply searching for the boy, whom we thought was hiding. The swing referred to is a piece of rope attached to a bough about eight of nine feet above the ground, having a piece of stick tied at the end of it. The stick was only a foot from the ground. It would not be a place to break one's neck, but I cannot say whether a boy would be killed if while he was swinging, he should fall on and knock his head on some hard substance like a stone. I stated that there were hairs on the mattock, they were on the edge of it, but no flesh. I heard the evidence given by Dr David Jones that he was very doubtful whether it was possible that the boys could have inflicted the injuries to the skull. I heard the evidence of Dr Arthur Jones to almost the same effect." PC John Williams, Pembrey, gave evidence as to conveying the prisoners' clothes to the analyst.

Dr William Morgan, Swansea, Analyst for the County of Carmarthen, said that on Saturday evening he received one flannel shirt, recently washed, one jacket and trousers, said to belong to David Mazey, one jacket and trousers and a left boot, said to belong to Benjamin Mazey. On Saturday evening he received one corduroy trousers, a flannel gown and an apron. These were damp and seemed to have been in water. He also received a bed sheet, which had, however, no trace of blood. He could find no satisfactory evidence on the gown or apron. The same remark applied to the trousers of the two boys. On the right and left sleeve wrists of Benjamin Mazey's jacket he could find no stains of blood. On the right cuff of David Mazey's jacket, he found evidence of blood, he also found blood on one of the two wrists of the flannel shirt. Below the knee of the damp corduroy trousers, he found what appeared to be blood. There was blood on the sole and nails of the boot. The caps had no trace of blood. On Thursday (10th) morning, he received from PC Wm. Thomas a pan of earth, in which was a quantity of coagulated blood.

Cross-examined by Mr Howell, he stated – "By the evidence of blood, I mean blood being present. I examined the clothes by chemical and microscopical tests. I cannot distinguish between human blood and the blood of any mammalia – that is any animal that sucks. I could not distinguish it from the blood of a rabbit. There was a total absence of blood on the clothes of Jane Mazey."

PC William Thomas, Pembrey, was the next witness to be called – "On Monday evening last, in company with PC William James, I was conveying the prisoners to Carmarthen goal. In the train, Jane Mazey asked PC James 'If he had not been at one time stationed at Pontarddulais'. He replied 'Yes'. She then said, 'I am quite innocent of this affair, I know nothing about it, God knows'. She added that she hoped the boys would say the truth about it, and addressing the boys, she said, 'You tell PC James all the truth about it'. Thereupon David Mazey said 'I saw John Thomas on Wednesday when he came into our house. Afterwards we went out to the garden to play with the swing. John Thomas and Benjamin got on top of the wall. John fell down on his head on the flags. After he fell he said – 'Oh, Dai bach, rhoi dy law' ('Oh dear, David, give me your hand'). I caught hold of his hand and he died directly'. Benjamin also stated, 'A piece of timber broke off the roof and John Thomas fell and I nearly fell too'. David continuing his statement said, 'I then caught hold of his hands and Benjamin his feet and we carried him to the top of the garden and placed some clods over him'. Benjamin said 'I only put one on him and I would not have done that if David had not told me to do so'. David continued: 'I then went into the house and carried some water from a tub and threw it on the blood. Something white came out of the head, I took that and threw it across the road into Mrs Gower's garden. On Thursday I went to search for the 'white thing' in the company of PS John Jones and on the garden hedge of Mrs Gower I found some brian – the brain that is now in methylated spirits'."

PC William James, Ferryside, corroborated the previous witness statement and added that he had heard David Mazey say, 'After I carried the body to the garden hedge, I took half-a-sovereign out of his trousers pocket. We afterwards divided it'. His mother had asked him why he had not told her before of it. He answered: 'I was afraid you would beat me'.

John Jones, Hall and Lock-up Keeper, said the prisoners were in his custody from Friday evening, February 4th, to Monday evening, February 7th. He stated – "I had a conversation with David on Friday in the presence of Benjamin Mazey and my son. He said 'I did not kill John Thomas, but he fell from an old roof'. He asked me whether he was to go home or to Carmarthen. He stated he had gone over part of the roof himself, from which John Thomas had fallen. 'When I came to where John Thomas was, I saw some little white thing coming out of his head, and 'Little Jack', (the deceased) said, Dai, Dai, Dai, three times and then died. After he was dead, I put my hand into his trouser pocket and took out the half-a-sovereign. We then carried him and buried him'. Benjamin said – 'It was not I that buried him but David'. I did not question the prisoners at all'.

Dr David Jones said – "The substance I saw at PS John Jones's house on Wednesday was brain, but of what kind I could not say. He told me where he found it."

Dr Jones, cross-examined by Mr Howell said – "I heard Dr J. A. Jones say at the inquest that it was doubtful whether the boys could have done it. I consider Dr Jones a skillful man and I fully agree with him. I think too, that it possible but improbable, that the injuries could have been done by them."

That closed the case for the prosecution.

No witnesses were called for the defence but Mr William Howell summed up giving a very impassioned address. He contended that the case against the woman had completely broken down, that there was no evidence against her, and asked the bench to take the story of the boys as a true explanation of the affair. Humanity and English Law assumed that children under 14 were incapable of crime unless it could be proved by clear unmistakable evidence that they had previously shown a precocious criminal disposition." . . . "This," he maintained, "the prosecution had not done."

Having retired for only about ten minutes, the bench returned and gave their verdict that after careful consideration they had determined to commit the prisoners for trial on a charge of wilfully murdering John Thomas.

THE MURDER TRIAL

Venue of the trial of Jane Mazey and her two boys was The Guildhall at Swansea and the appointed date of proceedings would be Thursday, 12th May, 1881. The indictment was the 'Wilful Murder of John Thomas' in February last.

The 'cause celebre' provoked a morbid atmosphere throughout the Principality and a huge crowd turned up at the courthouse on

The Town Hall. Swansea.

the eventful day. The hall was full to its utmost capacity and scores of onlookers failed to gain entry. A very warm day, combined with the heat of the crowded hall, resulted in furnace-like conditions, but despite this difficulty, the assembled group stayed there from 10 o'clock in the morning until the end of the trial a little before 8 o'clock in the evening. They persevered to remain because had they left the courtroom during that time they would not have been allowed to return.

The Kidwelly murder trial was the last case on the list for judicial examination on that day. Mr Justice Flave took his seat at the bench and made the comment that – ". . . it was a most extraordinary case as I ever remembered to have heard."

The dock was situated in the middle of the hall and the prisoners remained there during the trial. Jane Mazey's appearance had improved since the committal but from her demeanour it was apparent that she was fully aware of her seriously grave predicament and sobbed bitterly right through the whole of the proceedings. She kept her face turned down and seldom looked up; and due to her weak state and the imminence of her confinement she was allowed to remain seated. David, her elder son was next to her, his eyes just visible above the dock railings. He looked around quite freely and seemed to be as interested in the movements and speeches of the barristers as anyone present. Benjamin, the younger of the two brothers, was not to be seen above the railings but peered through them from time to time. He looked very tired and like his mother, kept his eyes down. The two boys were dressed in their own clothes. Occasionally, David looked into his mother's face and was ever ready when necessary to give her water, which she drank continuously. Towards the end of the trial Benjamin was sat down.

Jane Mazey, age 34, described as dressmaker, David Mazey, age 12 and Benjamin Mazey, age 10, were indicted for unlawfully and feloniously, and of malice, killing and murdering John Thomas, age 11 years, on the 2nd February last. Jane Mazey, the mother, also indicted as an accessory after the fact. All the prisoners pleaded "Not guilty."

Mr Bowen Q.C. and Mr Abel Thomas appeared for the prosecution, and Mr Bowen Rowlands appeared for the defence.

The Jury comprised Mr Griffith Llewellyn, then Mayor of Swansea, also representatives of the farming community and other members of the public. The elected foreman was Mr C. Fowler.

In his opening address, Mr Bowen, Q.C. prosecuting counsel, characterised the case as a most painful one. The law, he said, declared that persons under 8 years of age were incapable of committing murder, over 14 they were considered responsible for the crime of murder, but between the ages of 8 and 14 it was for the jury to decide. During counsel's summing up (facts of the tragedy), the prisoners kept up a stolid appearance although the mother drank water incessantly and showed signs of suffering and stress. The chain of circumstantial evidence, as given in detail by counsel, seemed to be overwhelmingly against all the prisoners.

Here, I will only briefly outline the proceedings as the evidence is a repetition of that given in the magisterial enquiry.

Mr Richard Williams, Surveyor and Architect of Burry Port, was called to give evidence. He had drawn up plans of the tragic scene, copies of which were in the hands of the jury and court. He spoke of the accuracy of the plan which made clear the surroundings where the tragedy occurred.

Mrs Mazey became extremely agitated and emotional when Mrs Ann Hughes gave her evidence – how that on the day following the tragedy, the female prisoner had denied John Thomas's entrance into her house, while she (Mrs Hughes) herself had sworn she had seen him go in.

Mother of the murdered child also gave evidence (in Welsh) and while doing so became very distraught, breaking down completely before cross-examination came to a close.

Mrs Margaret White, a shopkeeper with premises in Bridge Street, not having given evidence previously, said she had changed half-a-sovereign for one of the Mazey boys.

There was then a recess for lunch and when the court resumed, Benjamin was allowed to sit down.

Jane Mazey again showed great agitation when Police Sergeant John Jones stated that on charging the boy prisoners with the murder, they exclaimed they would never see their mother again.

The analyst's testimony was conclusive and he confirmed the presence of blood on the clothing of both the female prisoner and the boy prisoners.

At 5 o'clock his lordship consulted counsels and the jury on deciding whether to adjourn or carry through to conclude. It was decided to continue.

Mr Bowen, Q.C. prosecuting counsel, then began his address. He stated that in the case of murder, it was seldom that direct testimony could be brought against the accused and that in this case there was stronger evidence against the accused than in most cases of alleged murder. He reviewed the evidence given by the witnesses, taking the charge against the boys first, one by one overturning the theories of defence with regard to the supposed fall. He outlined the inconsistency of the stories told by the boys regarding the tragedy – that they were totally at variance with the facts given in evidence. Passing on to the mother, learned counsel stated that all the stories told by the female prisoner regarding the boy and the money in his possession, were contradictory. He wound up, imploring the jury not to shirk from their duty in considering their verdict in this case.

Mr Bowen Rowlands, defending counsel, began an impressive address by observing that the case was one of a most painful nature, not only because of the tender age of the deceased but also of those accused of killing him. He referred to the youth and presumptive weakness of the boy prisoners and endeavoured to impress upon the jury the fallacy of presumption or circumstantial evidence. He then went over the evidence, and with regard to the female prisoner, reminded the jury that the day after the boy's death she did all she could to trace the money known to be in the boy's possession. She went into the town, leaving the house in the occupancy of the police sergeant and Evan Thomas, father of the missing boy, giving them uninterrupted opportunity to question the young boys. "Does this seem like the action of a guilty person, someone with something to hide? I think not," he said. Turning to the evidence of the doctors, he charged that the injuries found on the deceased boy's head were caused by a fall.

Having taken over an hour to deliver his impassioned address, counsel finally sat down.

The female prisoner was deeply affected during the address, the boys showed no emotion whatsoever, they simply looked around as if they were the least implicated persons present.

In summing up, his lordship stated that in the charges of murder against children of the age of the accused, the law not only required that sufficient proof of the actual deed should be forthcoming, but that the accused had sufficient knowledge of the enormity of the offence. He then carefully reviewed the evidence and the proceedings came to an end. The jury were expected to take quite some time to consider their verdict, but the emphatic warnings of Mr Bowen Rowlands and the Judge – "not to return a verdict of guilty unless they were perfectly convinced of the prisoners' guilt" – had apparently enabled them to easily make up their minds. The jury retired at twenty-five minutes to eight o'clock and returned five minutes later when Mr Fowler, the foreman, announced a verdict of 'Not Guilty'.

The crowd gathered in the court showed no reaction at all when the verdict was declared, except for Jane Mazey who burst into tears. The two boys, if they were at all affected, did not show it. However, they listened and watched with great interest the foreman of the jury being questioned, as if they realized what an important part of their lives were those few moments.

In the streets of Swansea the main topic of conversation was the unexpected result.

The prisoners were discharged immediately but did not leave Swansea until the following day. They caught the train for Kidwelly accompanied by the husband of the woman, father of the two boys, who had attended at the court to follow the dramatic proceedings.

The Mazeys moved away from Kidwelly – a wise decision – and in their best interests as general feeling in the town was complete and utter surprise at the final course of events.

Worthy of comment perhaps is a press report stating that photographs of the most significant places where the murder happened, were selling at good prices. Gruesome or what!!

9

Local Coronation Celebrations

July 1820 – Coronation of King George IV
The Rev. C. W. Bowen with helpers entertained children to an excellent dinner at the National School on the day of the Coronation of King George IV.

In the evening about 20 gentlemen from the vicinity sat down to a dinner at the Pelican Inn, Rev. Bowen in the chair. The worthy mayor called innumerable loyal toasts and the party went on until a rather late hour. The bells of St Mary's Church rang a merry peal nearly all day.

June 1838 – Coronation of Queen Victoria
As a token of esteem and respect, the day of youthful Queen Victoria's Coronation, began with the ringing of church bells.

Mayor Ald. D. Williams of Coleman, the Custodian of the Castle, Mr Jones of Parc-y-Box, and several influential and respected citizens of the town, met at the Pelican Inn in the evening and long before nightfall many a cheerful glass had been taken to celebrate this auspicious day when 18-year-old Victoria stood on the very threshold of her accession to the throne.

Queen Victoria, 1837-1901.
(Photograph: Author).

CORONATION OF KING EDWARD VII, 1902

Thursday, 26th June, 1902

A full programme of events had been arranged in Kidwelly to celebrate the Coronation. News of the king's sudden illness and postponement of the crowning ceremony came as a shock to the Principality and a decision was made to cancel all proposed celebrations. In consequence, on Thursday, 26th June, the planned enthronement timetable was superseded by well attended prayer meetings for the king's recovery. Petitionary prayers took place at Morfa and Horeb Calvinistic Chapels and also at Bethesda Welsh Wesleyan Chapel. At 11 o'clock a solemn service of intercession, attended by the

King Edward VII, 1901-10.
(Photograph: Author).

Mayor and most members of the council, was held at the Parish Church. The service was conducted by the Rev. D. Daven Jones.

Saturday, 9th August, 1902

News of a new date in August for the Coronation brought great relief and the appointed special committee met to confirm arrangements of the original programme. It was decided to present all the schoolchildren with commemorative mugs and confirmed that the day would be rigidly observed as a half-day holiday with all the shops, etc. closing at 1 o'clock. The public would be asked to decorate their houses and streets, and to please do their shopping on the Friday.

Coronation Day

Festivities took place in regal style, commencing with an impressive service at St Mary's Church. The Rev. Hugh Rees, Curate, conducted the service and Mr J. Morgan played the harmonium. Later on in the morning, a group of women visited all the aged and deserving poor of the town and gave a gift of half-a-crown to each one.

Procession

Everyone taking part in the pageant met at Hillfield at 1.30 p.m. and lined up to form a procession. The parade was headed by a contingent of boys from Castle School, one of them dressed in majestic regalia fitting to the role-play of a king, riding in a carriage and attended by horsemen and courtiers. Britannia was represented in the appropriate distinctive outfit and girls from Hillfield School were dressed in national costume – Welsh, English, Irish and Scottish. All the schoolchildren carried flags, and especially enjoyed all the hurly burly and excitement. The Mayor and Corporation, and members of public associations joined in to parade the main streets which were bedecked with colourful bunting, streamers and flags. When the parade was over, the children made their way to various schools and were entertained to a Coronation tea. The children from Mynydd-y-Garreg arrived by 'gambos' loaned by farmers in the locality to enjoy their celebration party in the Town Hall.

Mrs Griffiths of London House kindly loaned Hillfield to hold a sports event which commenced at 4 o'clock. The competitions went on until 8 o'clock and then a carnival got under way. Prizes were handed out at both sports and carnival events. When darkness fell, thousands of fairy lights and chinese lanterns were lit to twinkle and glow in the inky night sky to add a magic ambience to the jubilations. A glittering fireworks display went off with a bang (pun unintended) and lasted for about an hour – a grand finale to a most memorable day.

An enthusiastic committee with John Morgan and D. O. Jones serving as hon. secs. and W. Young as treasurer, had worked very hard to make the day such a huge success. They could be well pleased with the result of their efforts.

Town Mayor, Ald. J. G. Anthony, was one of the elite guests invited to Westminster Abbey to witness the splendour of the Coronation Ceremony. Before leaving for London, he and the Mayoress visited all the schools to present the Coronation mugs.

Coronation Memorial

The town clock, out of commission since the lightning strike of 1884, was at last repaired at the expense of the Borough Council. It was decided that the council would also meet the extra costs necessary to raise the dials to a higher elevation, this to be considered a lasting memorial to the Coronation of Edward VII.

CORONATION OF KING GEORGE V AND QUEEN MARY, 1911

May 1911 – Celebrations
The Borough Council, Mayor W. D. James in the chair, resolved to donate £50 towards the expected costs of celebrating King George V's Coronation. It was proposed to call a meeting to include representatives of the council, various churches and chapels of the town, and two teachers from each school to discuss arrangements for the celebrations.

June 1911 – Fireworks
Dr Tommy Griffiths of Henblas, Bridge Street, made known his

King George V, 1910-36.
(Photograph: Author).

intention to set up a display of fireworks on Coronation night at Hillfield. This was not part of the official programme but simply by reason of his kind disposition, a generous contribution to the festivites.

June 1911, Thursday 22nd – Coronation Day
The celebrations began with special services at St Mary's Parish Church conducted by the Rev. Gruffydd Evans, and at Morfa CM Chapel led by the Rev. W. C. Jenkins. Schoolchildren, boy scouts, members of the Borough Council, ministers and clergy turned up at 2.30 p.m. to form a procession at the Hillfield School. The Town Band led the impressive parade and Mynydd-y-Garreg Silver Band brought up the rear. Nearly every child carried a flag and bubbling over with excitement waved them merrily as they went on their way. The route and indeed all parts of the town had been lavishly decorated with brightly coloured bunting and garlands.

Mrs Davies of the Plough Inn received an award for the best business premises display and the Park Villa residence of Mrs Williams was acclaimed the best dressed individual house. Messrs Davies Bros of London House, Bridge Street, excelled at night time with their premises brightly illuminated with a crown and the letters G and M prominent in their patriotic display. Hundreds of yards of gaily coloured streamers and bunting fluttered all over Broomhill, and Rumsey House also stood out with myriads of rainbow coloured streamers dancing and bobbing to match the blithe atmosphere of the festive day. National flags were unfurled to fly proudly on the buildings at the Brick Works, the Railway Station and Mountain View.

Various schools in the town arranged special teas for the children, the Morfa Vestry being the venue for the Mynydd-y-Garreg young people. True to the bane of the West Wales climate, heavy rain fell and the sports event was postponed until the following Saturday. The rain cleared at about 8.30 p.m. and at 10 o'clock Dr Griffiths hosted a magnificent fireworks display at Hillfield. The land had been loaned by Mr Davies of London House where a large crowd had gathered to enjoy the illuminescent show.

KING GEORGE VI AND QUEEN ELIZABETH, 1937

April 1937
A Coronation dance was held at the Church of England School in Pendre – first, to celebrate the coronation and, secondly to raise cash for the renovation fund. The school had been appropriately decorated with flags and bunting in the biased nationally favoured red, white and blue coloured fairy lights. MCs for the evening were P. R. Squire of Kymers Villa and the Rev. D. Daven Thomas, BA, curate of St Mary's Church in Swansea (a former Kidwelly boy). Everyone enjoyed the well organised ebullient as well as the more leisurely style of dancing and prizes were handed out for fancy dress.

King George VI, 1936-52.
(Photograph: Author).

Coronation Week Festivities
Tuesday, May 11th

Nurse Morgan, a popular Kidwelly District Nurse, received a coronation gift at a pre-planned get-together at Trinity English Methodist Church schoolroom. The Committee of Kidwelly and District Child and Welfare and Maternity Clinic presented the nurse with a bureau in recognition of her valuable services. The gathering of friends and colleagues included Town Mayor Cllr. D. G. Evans and Mrs Evans, and the Clinic's Medical Officer, Dr D. Beynon Davies of the Barbican. The mayoress, chairperson of the committee, presented the well deserved honour.

Tuesday Evening, May 11th

A well supported coronation supper at Siloam Baptist Chapel vestry was a great success. The tables were bursting at the seams with a variety of food, and the Minister, the Rev. H. R. Jones, thanked the ladies who had worked so hard to prepare and serve the savoury and sweet refreshments. He also thanked the large number that had turned up to partake of the soiree.

Coronation Day – Wednesday, May 12th

First and foremost at 9 a.m. a Public Service of Thanksgiving was held at Capel Sul Independent Chapel, and a large congregation also graced the occasion. Town Mayor, Cllr. D. G. Evans, was present, accompanied by the Deputy Mayor, Cllr. Gomer Morris, and members and officials of the Borough Council. The service was conducted by the Rev. E. J. Herbert, (Morfa), the Rev. H. R. Jones (Siloam), the Rev. A. C. Pearce (late Welsh Wesleyans), the Rev. D. M. Davies (Curate) and the Rev. E. J. Kingsbury (Vicar) who delivered the address. The organist was Cllr. Henry John Owen. All the streets in the town, the houses and business premises were festooned with flowers, chains of streamers, bunting and flags which helped to sustain a happy holiday mood.

Tea Parties

Schoolchildren assembled at their respective schools at 4 p.m. to attend sumptuous tea parties. The rooms had been beautifully decorated for the occasion and the teaching staff willingly took on a new role of waiter/waitress to serve at the abundantly food-laden tables. However, helpers were at hand to support if and when required. When the tea party was over, each child was presented with the usual conventional mug. Another item on the agenda was a parade on the cheerfully emblazoned streets, headed by Mynydd-y-Garreg Silver Band, resplendent in their smart brand new uniforms. Friends, neighbours and relatives lining the parade route were enthralled at the sight of so many 'little darlings' marching together and waving hundreds of miniature Union Jacks as they went by.

Sports and Fireworks
When the parade eventually arrived at Park Stephens, the customary sports event took off and the band played some well-known melodies to entertain the spectators. When darkness fell, people gathered to watch a spectacular fireworks display.

Coronation Dance
The memorable day was brought to an end with a coronation dance at the Town Hall. Norman Maliphant and his band provided foot-tapping music and John Morgan of Water Street, who was MC, ensured a diversity of music so everyone could enjoy a jolly evening.

Floodlighting
Throughout the week floodlights were beamed onto the Norman Castle, the ancient Church and the War Memorial, producing an ethereal fairytale appearance to the whole town.

Cash Gifts
All babies born during this eventful coronation week, were presented with a gift of five shillings and the babies born on Coronation Day received one whole pound.

Coronation Eisteddfod – 15th May
Mr Elvet Fisher, Hon. Sec., reported that a large crowd had supported the Eisteddfod held at Welsh Wesleyan Chapel. Henry John Owen, a well qualified musician, was accompanist to the competitors and Mr Fisher said the competition had been of a very high standard.

London Trip – Saturday, 15th May
Staff and employees of Messrs Stephens Silica Brick Company Ltd., travelled by train to London on a sightseeing tour of the ornate and elaborate displays and illuminations in the capital city. Sir Alfred Stephens, JP, of Broomhill, generously met the costs and at the railway station he, Lady Stephens and daughter, Miss Audrey Stephens, saw

the party off. The trippers were escorted by Ald. T. W. Thomas, General Manager at the Brick Works. Several Kidwelly expatriots, who had made London their home, met the group at Paddington Station to enjoy the day together, the weary tourists left the fair city at 1.45 a.m. on the Sunday morning.

CORONATION OF QUEEN ELIZABETH II AND PRINCE PHILIP

List of planned events for week commencing 31st May, 1953

Sunday, May 31st	Religious Service at Kidwelly Castle, weather permitting.
	Capel Sul if wet weather prevails.
	Community Carol Service at Morfa C.M. Chapel.
Monday, June 1st	Coronation Whist Drive.
	Street Cricket Finals.
Tuesday, June 2nd	Street Tea Parties.
Coronation Day	Coronation Beacon at Mynydd-y-Garreg (evening).
Wednesday, June 3rd	'Go-as-you-please' concert.
	Children's Coronation Tea Party.
Thursday, June 4th	Coronation Dog Show at the Town Hall.
	Band Concert at the Town Hall.
Friday, June 6th	Finals Six-a-side Soccer Competition.
	Crowning ceremony Miss Kidwelly.
Saturday, June 6th	Coronation Carnival and Sports.
	Coronation Dance at the Castle.

In Kidwelly it was a case of 'all systems go' to celebrate the coronation of Queen Elizabeth II. On Sunday afternoon town dignitaries Mayor and Mayoress Ald. and Mrs John Rees, Borough Councillors and officials, a detachment from the Royal Air Force Pembrey Squadron, local Police Constabulary led by Sgt. T. C. Allen, members of the clergy and various other organisations, formed a procession led by Mynydd-y-Garreg Silver Band and made their way to Capel Sul for a special coronation service. Mayor's chaplain the Rev. E. J. Kingsbury officiated at the chapel which was chock-a-block with such a large congregation. In the evening a full house at Morfa C.M. Chapel enjoyed a session of hymn singing.

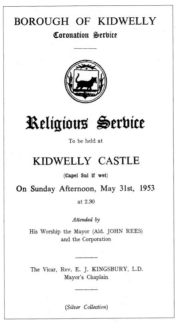

BOROUGH OF KIDWELLY
Coronation Service

Religious Service

To be held at

KIDWELLY CASTLE

(Capel Sul if wet)

On Sunday Afternoon, May 31st, 1953

at 2.30

Attended by

His Worship the Mayor (Ald. JOHN REES)
and the Corporation

The Vicar, Rev. E. J. KINGSBURY, L.D.
Mayor's Chaplain

(Silver Collection)

(Courtesy Mrs Margaret Hughes).

Finals of the street cricket competition took place on Monday with a tension-packed Whist Drive being held in the evening.

Tuesday was the all important Coronation Day. Street parties had been organised but again, due to our unstable weather in West Wales, it became necessary to find alternative venues to shelter from obstructive annoying rain. Even so, everyone enjoyed the delicious fare prepared by the women who had worked hard – cooking, baking, setting out and serving at tables, and the results were a credit to them all. Each child was presented with a bag of sweets and a souvenir to mark the Coronation of Her Majesty Queen Elizabeth II and everyone it seems had a marvellous time. Tea parties such as these went on all week and the Mayor and Coronation Committee went on a walk-about to visit each party.

With the advent of a new media phenomenon, sensational television transmission in Kidwelly made revolutionary changes and inroads in the way important events were presented. For the very first time in history the public were able to see the enthronement of a monarch while the event was actually taking place. They saw the beauty and splendour of the procession and the Queen in her golden coach on

The crowned Queen.
(Photograph: Author).

Kidwelly's headmaster deputy mayor, Mr Hefin Evans, with children during their celebration tea.
(Photograph courtesy *Llanelly Star*, 1953).

her way to renowned Westminster Abbey; they saw the solemn and dignified ritual connected with ancient coronation ceremonies, and the delighted crowds all along the route, waving and cheering the queen and other high ranking members of the royal family.

Naturally, everyone was eager to see the high-tone enthronement ceremony made possible by the amazing feat of electronics efficiency. Kind neighbours who were proud owners of small 12-14 inch sets (primitive compared with today's modern high tech megalithic units) improvised seating and space to host friends and relatives so they could see the results of this amazing piece of resourceful equipment. On coronation day people in Kidwelly spent many hours eyes glued to the screen as the magnificent proceedings unfolded before their very eyes. A wonderful and very acceptable innovation, especially for the housebound.

In the evening a large crowd congregated at the top of Mynydd-y-Garreg to see Kidwelly Scouts launch a volley of rocket missiles and set alight a coronation bonfire. The blazing beacon could be seen for miles around.

Wednesday was set apart by the Borough Council to entertain all the children in the borough to tea and scrumptious cakes, and each child received sweets and the familiar acceptable mug. Following on from the tea party the children were steered into a procession carrying mini Union Jacks and led by Mynydd-y-Garreg Silver Band marched resolutely to the castle. On arriving they were given delicious ice-cream and there followed happy-go-lucky dancing on the green, music being provided by the band.

1953 Coronation Street Tea Party at Hillfield Villas.
(Photograph courtesy Mrs Ann Jones).

In the evening a 'Go-as-you-please' concert proved to be a success being well attended by an encouraging and talented audience. A truly enjoyable evening.

Thursday, singled out for animal lovers, again proved to be in the order of a successfully entertaining contest and in the evening a tightly packed Town Hall enjoyed a Band Concert provided by the Mynydd-y-Garreg musicians.

The final rounds of the six-a-side soccer competition took place at Park Stephens on Friday evening. In the quarter-finals, two sides from the RAF Station at Pembrey and two sides from Kidwelly were knocked out. The semi-final results were – Llansaint 3, Carway 1, Trimsaran 6, Meinciau 1. In a cracking final, Llansaint finally edged out Trimsaran by 3 goals to 2 to win the trophy. Mayor Ald. John Rees presented the runners-up award to Trimsaran's captain Ivor Roberts. He then called on Llansaint skipper Ivor Jones to collect the winning trophy. Ivor Jones thanked every team for an excellent contest, and he thanked his team mates with a special tribute to Delme Davies for a first-class display.

On Friday evening in the Pavilion at Park Stephens the town's own crowning ceremonies took place. Mayor Ald. John Rees crowned Miss Joy Daniels of Hillfield Villas, Miss Kidwelly; and Mayoress Mrs Rees crowned little Eryl Griffiths of Station Road, Fairy Queen.

The Royal British Legion had organised a Coronation Fête and Gala for Saturday and almost every house in the town had been decorated with flags and bunting in a kaleidoscope of colours. Crowds of people in festive mood lined the procession route as the fancy dress pageant, headed by the Mynydd-y-Garreg Silver Band, wound their way around the town. The parade returned to Park Stephens for the habitual sports competition and local schoolchildren demonstrated their skill at folk dancing.

In the evening a Coronation Dance in the grounds of the floodlit Norman Castle, music provided by the Rhythmic Quartet, Kidwelly, brought the memorable action-packed week to a gratifying conclusion.

Miss Joy Daniels, 23, Hillfield Villas, the borough's choice as 'Miss Kidwelly', for the local festivities.
(Photograph courtesy Llanelly Star, 1953).

10.

Religion

A LIST OF PRIORS OF THE BENEDICTINE PRIORY OF KIDWELLY

Abraham	circa 1240
Gervase	1268
Galfridus de Coker	1301
Robert Dunsterr	1346
John Flode	1361
Philip Morevyle	1399
John De Kidwellye	1404
Robert Fyfhyde	1428
John Caunvell	1438
John Sherborne	1482
John Hestrige	1487
John Whitchurch	1520
John Godmyster	1537

Note: The Priors were also the Rectors of the Parish Church of St Mary. The Priory was founded before 1115 by Roger, Bishop of Salisbury, as a cell of Sherborne Abbey in Dorset.

(W. Hill Morris papers)

Kidwelly was one of a number of little priories founded by the Normans in South Wales. The monks associated with Kidwelly seem to have been of the Sherborne Order originating from Dorset in the West of England. The number of residents were very small, appearing never to have been more than a prior and one or two monks. The priory served as the parish church of the borough.

Ffynnon Fair – St Mary's Well, 2003.
(Photograph: Author).

Ffynnon Fair

I was overjoyed that after some astute detective work I have redis-
covered the ancient well known as St Mary's Well (Ffynnon Fair). It
is located some 500 yards north of the castle in marshy ground near
the Gwendraeth Fach River. A friend and I cleaned up the site and
we were delighted to witness the cool waters continuing to flow as
they did almost a thousand years ago, when the Normans invaded
our country.

By far the most popular of wells dedicated to non-Celtic saints
was Our Lady whose wells are found in all parts of Europe. Her name
appears in connection with Welsh wells in a variety of forms, such
as Mair (Fair), Mary or Our Lady. In a great number of cases, where
the name Ffynnon Fair occurs, the parish church will be dedicated
to St Mary, as at Kidwelly. She was a favourite saint of the Normans
– the majority of her wells are to be found in districts where the
Norman Anglo influence was strongest.

Underground wells were regarded as places of magic and mystery
where strange forces were at work. There were 'holy wells', 'healing
wells' and 'wishing wells', and rituals associated with wells and
sacred springs can be identified way back into the mists of time.

Pilgrimages were made to Ffynnon Fair near our Kidwelly Castle on Lady Day, and folk would drink the water and throw pins into the well for good luck. These wells were considered sacrosanct and the waters were said to be purer than the waters of other wells.

1200s – Exposed Church
On the foundation of the Priory of Kidwelly, the church of St Ishmael was appropriated to it and continued to do so until the Dissolution. The right to present to the parish of St Ishmael the apportionment of a priest rested with the prior. In old documents it was called Llan Ishmael and claims to be one of the oldest churches in Wales.

Saint Ishmael's church

The church consists of a chancel, nave, north aisle, south transept and a square tower emplaced against the south wall toward the western end. The earlier building dates back to the 13th century, when the church comprised a single-chambered edifice. The usual late 14th or early 15th century extensions provided a north aisle and possibly the south transeptal chapel.

St Ishmael's Church is situated on a very exposed area of the coastline, not many yards from the shore but sufficiently high above the sea to place it beyond the direct impact of the waves.

1578 – Mediaeval Chapel
Capel Teilo was situated two miles north of the town near Mynydd-y-Garreg and is recorded on Speed's 1578 Map of Carmarthenshire. A symbol to identify a church or chapel marks the exact site.

1713 – House of God
A very old entrance door to St Mary's Church is now door to the tower. It bears the Latin inscription: 'HAEC EST DOMUS DEI PORTA COELI' ('This is the House of God, the Gateway to Heaven').

July, 1764 – John Wesley
On Tuesday, 31st July, John Wesley, the Methodist Minister/Founder preached at Kidwelly en route to Gower. An account in his personal diary reads – "An honest man of Kidwelly told us there was no difficulty in riding the sands, so we rode on. In ten minutes one overtook us who used to guide persons over, and it was well he did or in all probability we had been swallowed up. The whole sands are at least ten miles over, with many streams of quicksand, but our guide was thoroughly acquainted with them.

1797 – Castle Farm
Members of the Baptist church, as far back as 1797, met in the farmhouse of Mr Harries, Castle Farm, for prayer meetings and services. When the congregation increased, Mr Harries donated land (previously

Siloam Baptist Chapel, 1821. It was built facing the castle.
(Photograph courtesy Siloam Baptist Chapel).

an orchard located opposite the farmhouse), on which to erect a chapel. The chapel was officially opened in 1821.

1816 June – Shadow of the Castle
The Wesleyan cause thrived in Kidwelly and it became necessary for its followers to build a chapel. In 1816 Bethesda Chapel (Welsh Wesleyan), a simple box-like structure was erected in the shadow of the ancient castle and was officially opened for worship on June 9th. Bethesda was instrumental in strengthening the Wesleyan movement in the town, and it was a sad day when the last tangible link with it vanished when the chapel in Kidwelly was demolished in 1962.

1867 – Worthy Collection
The Rev. W. C. Jenkins, the newly installed minister of Capel Sul, organised and delivered a very interesting lecture in aid of this worthwhile cause. A large crowd attended and the substantial proceeds of the worthy collection were donated to the widow of the late minister, Rev. David Jones.

July 1886 – School Room
The Welsh Methodists in Kidwelly resolved to provide a Sunday School and the elders of Morfa Welsh Calvinistic Chapel decided a separate school room was desirable. Building work commenced and in July 1886 the vestry was officially opened, and became the ideal site for the activities of young members of the chapel.

1887 – Dr Joseph Parry
The hymn tune, 'Cydweli', was written in 1887 by Dr Joseph Parry, probably in fond memory of his mother, Elizabeth Parry, who had died in 1886.

Joseph Parry was one of Wales' greatest musicians – ". . . heb amheuaeth, y Cymro mwyaf adnabyddus yn y byd ar ddechrau'r ugeinfed ganrif" – he wrote over 400 hymns, including 'Aberystwyth' and 'Sirioldeb'; he composed the first Welsh opera, 'Hywel a Blodwen', oratorios such as 'Iesu o Nazareth' and, of course, 'Myfanwy'. He was the first Professor of Music at Aberystwyth University.

Our interest in 'Y Doctor Mawr' is fuelled by the fact that his mother, Elizabeth Parry (née Richards), was born in the Graig Farm, Cydweli, circa 1805. Joseph certainly inherited her musical talent for she was an accomplished *penillion* singer and had a beautiful

Bethesda Chapel. Late 1950s.
(Photograph courtesy Peter Evans).

contralto voice. She probably led the singing at Capel Sul in Ferry Road, where she and her family were members. Her baptism records are still at Capel Sul.

Unfortunately, like so many young men and women of the time, Bet (as she was known) joined the mass exodus from the country-side to the booming industrial community of Merthyr Tydfil. She left

Hymn – 'Cydweli' written by Dr Joseph Parry.
(Courtesy Mrs Janice Rowlands).

the Graig in 1820 and went as a serving maid to Methusalem Jones, minister of Bethesda Chapel. There, she recited and led the singing with Martha Thomas.

At Bethesda she met and married Daniel Parry from Pembroke, a finer in the Cyfarthfa iron works.

After the marriage, the family moved to Chapel Row, Cyfarthfa, now preserved as an ironworker's cottage. She had eight children, five of whom survived to adulthood, and the third to be born was Joseph Parry (May 24th, 1841).

She must have been a remarkable woman: she coped with the move from rural Cydweli to the industrial cauldron of Merthyr Tydfil and now Daniel, together with thousands of others, decided to emigrate to Pennsylvania to work in the 'Rough and Ready Mill'. For the year she was left behind, Bet coped with her family and five lodgers who helped to boost the income. In 1854 she and her family sailed after her husband on the *Jane Anderson*, a voyage of six weeks and two days.

She became an American citizen and after Daniel's death in 1866, Bet moved to live with her daughter, Jane in Plymouth. Then in 1882, she went to live with her daughter Betsy in Maine. Dr Parry wrote the hymn tune 'Maine' in memory of Bet after her death and also wrote a ballad dedicating it to his beloved mother – 'Mam':

> "Mournful news that mournful card brought me from
>   a distant shore
> Mother dead, and O how hard seemed the parting
>   ere more."

Despite our lack of knowledge of what happened to Elizabeth's family at Graig Farm (for they are not included in the 1961 census), nothing can diminish Cydweli's treasured connection with one of Wales' greatest musicians, Dr Joseph Parry and his very talented and redoubtable mother, Elizabeth Parry.

(Mrs Janice Rowlands)

May 1902 – A Dedication by the Lord Bishop
The Lord Bishop of St David's solemnly dedicated a new altar and reredos, and a new peal of six bells in St Mary's Church. The new furniture was made of solid oak and the old altar was removed and transferred to the side chapel. Assisting the bishop were Rev. D.

Daven Jones and his curate Rev. Hugh Rees. Later on when the service was over tea was served in the Parish Room.

July 1904 – Japanese Fête
Saturday was a gala day in Kidwelly as members of the church organised a Japanese Garden Fête and Café Chantant in the castle grounds. The castle was beautifully decorated in gay colours and flags enhanced the towers. A brass band played, the stalls exuded a pleasant oriental flavour and the lady helpers, dressed in Japanese costume, instigated a delightful authenticity to the eastern ethos of the festivities. The stalls offered sweets, curries, fortune telling, art displays, a museum and refreshments. During the day 800 people had visited the castle and the event was a huge success. The Rev. D. Daven Jones thanked everyone who had taken part and announced that all the profits would be devoted to church work in the parish.

1919 – Apostolic Church
The Apostolic Church in Kidwelly came into being in 1919. The Thomas family, fervent members of the Apostolic calling, took up residence at Coleman Farm where meetings were held at their farm-house. In the 1940s a room was hired at the Pelican Hotel (now Borough Offices) as the farmhouse by then was too small to accommodate the growing congregation. That room now houses the Town Library.

March 1922 – Memorial Service
A memorial service was held at St Teilo's Church, Mynydd-y-Garreg, when a brass altar cross together with a brass altar lectern and a new altar frontal were unveiled by Miss Dorothy Thomas, Velindre House, on behalf of her father, John Thomas, who was ill and unable to attend. The cross bears the following inscription –

> "1914-1918: To the Glory of God and in memory of R. J. Anderson, W. J. Anthony, D. J. Howells, W. H. Lewis, A. Styles. R.I.P."

Messrs Morgan Bros., Undertakers, presented a beautiful oak table in memory of their brother John Morgan, a former mayor of the town. Mrs Davies of the Plough & Harrow Inn, presented two lectern frontals, a Welsh Bible and a Prayer Book with which to furnish the altar.
The vicar, Rev. D. Ambrose Jones, assisted by the Rev. Curzon

Jones, Curate and the Rev. J. J. Davies, Vicar of St Maelog's Church, Llandefeilog, conducted the dedication service.

1924 – Wireless Concert
A Grand Bazaar and Sale of Work was held at Rumsey House, organised by the Capel Sul Congregational Chapel. A variety of stalls had been prepared and a wireless concert attracted large crowds. All money raised to augment the chapel building fund. Opening ceremonies were performed by Sir Alfred Stephens J.P. on the Tuesday and Mrs David Evans of Whitchurch on the Wednesday.

1926 – Bachelor's Party
A very successful Bachelor's Tea Party (the first of its kind) was held at Capel Sul organised and arranged by the Capel Sul Debating Society. Tables were laden and well laid out with delicious fare. A concert took place after the tea, with Henry John Owen, a musician of Ramleth, being the accompanist.

1927 – Eynon's Charabanc
At the kind invitation of E. H. Stephens, 80 members of the English Wesleyan School travelled by Mr Eynon's charabanc on their annual outing to Coedybrain in Ferryside. The tea was most enjoyable but because rain stole a march on the day, a decision was made to hold the sports event at Pant-y-Cox the following week.

September 1937 – Organist
Miss Grace Gravell was appointed church organist, succeeding Mr David Thomas, Penybryn, who had given 40 years of faithful service since taking up the post in July 1897. Miss Gravell had been deputy organist for the previous nine years and was a gifted and accomplished musician.

1937 – Divine Service
On Kidwelly's traditional 'Mayor Sunday', Cllr. D. G. Evans, J.P. who had been re-elected leader of the council, attended a divine service at Morfa Chapel. A large procession headed by the Mynydd-y-Garreg Silver Band progressed to the chapel where the Mayor's Chaplain, the Rev. E. J. Herbert, conducted the service.

December 1948 – New Cemetery
The new public cemetery in Ferry Road was consecrated on a Sunday

Town Cemetery, 2003.
(Photograph: Author).

by the Rev. E. J. Kingsbury, Vicar, assisted by the Rev. W. A. Jenkins, Capel Sul, the Rev. W. O. Williams, Siloam and the Rev. G. D. Jones, Morfa. Also present were the Town Mayor and Officials of the Corporation. The public burial ground was badly needed as space in the church and chapels was very limited.

1975 – Consecration
June 1975 was an important day for the followers of the Roman Catholic faith in the town. A new church named 'Our Lady and St Cadoc' was consecrated by Bishop L. D. Fox. A Latin inscription on a handmade wood plaque to commemorate the consecration reads – 'LAUS DEO SAMPER' (Glory to God Always).

RUMSEY HOUSE CONVERTED INTO A CHAPEL

Rumsey House was constructed and given its name in 1862 by T. W. A. Evans (1841-97), an architect who was later appointed Mayor of Kidwelly, and eventually it became the home of Harold Greenwood. The Independent Congregationalists, who held their meetings

Capel Sul, 1785-1926.
The Rev. Wm. Castellau Jenkins (1882-1924), Minister 1867-1919.
The Old Ferry Road Chapel.
(Photograph courtesy Capel Sul Chapel).

at that time in their Ferry Road Chapel, bought Rumsey House in 1923 and the building was converted by J. Morgan of Carmarthen during the years 1924-26. The ground floor was modified and became the schoolroom and the two upper floors were merged, redesigned and converted to become a chapel.

31st August, 1923
Rumsey House, one of the bigger mansions in Kidwelly, was sold for £1,525. Kidwelly Council did consider purchasing but failed to make a deal.

Mr T. B. Gravell recalls his late father-in-law, Mr Jack Edwards (Jack-y-Bwlch), saying that following acquittal of his wife's murder, Harold Greenwood approached Mr Edwards and other borough councillors too, asking: "What is the Council doing about buying Rumsey House?"

30th November, 1923
A two-day sale of furniture and fittings, etc. at Rumsey House attracted a crowd of buyers and good prices were realised.

June 1924

A bazaar and wireless show was held in the grounds of Rumsey House which had been acquired for the purpose of converting into a chapel. In addition to the usual stalls there was a wireless concert and children's entertainment. All proceeds went to the Chapel of Capel Sul.

March 1926

Capel Sul Dramatic Society held a splendid Welsh drama, supervised by the minister, Rev. E. Curig Davies, and chaired by the Mayor, Cllr. E. J. Gower. The event drew a large crowd and all proceeds went to the Chapel Building Fund.

OPENING OF A NEW CHAPEL

Sunday, April 25th, 1926, was a red letter day for the congregation-alists in Kidwelly when their visions and ambitions came to fruition. Members of the chapel had decided two and a half years previously to purchase the premises known as Rumsey House for conversion into a chapel. The mansion was placed in the capable hands of Messrs David Jones & Sons, Contractors of Carmarthen, and Mr J. Howard Morgan, Architect, also of Carmarthen, who transformed the building to become one of the finest chapels in the area. The minister was the Rev. Curig Davies, the secretary Mr Wesley Reynolds and the treasurer Mr W. H. Williams.

The Kidwelly members had worshipped in the chapel at Ferry Road for over 150 years and on this particular Sunday, they all met and held a short service there. When the service was over, the congregation formed a procession and led by the Rev. Curig Davies, and Elder members David Davies and Morris Davies who carried the Books of the Sanctuary, walked quietly to their new place of worship.

At the entrance of Capel Sul (formerly Rumsey House) Mr George Jones, Boro' Stores, handed the key of the main door to the chapel's senior deacon, Mr William Wilkins, while Mr G. H. Evans, precentor, handed the key of the inner door to Miss Frances Gower, a senior member of the congregation. The keys were a gift to the recipients from the chapel members in commemoration of this important opening event. The service was conducted by the Rev. E. Curig Davies, assisted by Messrs William Evans and D. B. Protheroe (students and members of the chapel). The minister delivered an inspiring sermon followed by celebration of the Holy Communion.

Capel Sul and Town Bridge, 2003.
(Photograph: Author).

On Sunday evening the Rev. Robert Jones, Sardis, Trimsaran, delivered his sermon as did the Rev. W. Davies, Pontyates, and the local Male Voice Party, under their conductor Stephen H. Evans, sang beautiful appropriate hymns during the service.

The official opening took place on Tuesday morning, April 27th, and the celebratory service was introduced by the Rev. Samuel Jones of Llandaff. The Rev. E. Curig Davies said that "... the members had looked forward to this day, having had a hard struggle to leave the old chapel, where the cause had been so well mounted for the last 141 years, as in the time when the present flourishing town of Llanelly was known and spoken of as being near Kidwelly" ... "They," added the minister, "did not desire to abandon the old tradition, but through having the Books of the Sanctuary from the old chapel, a link would be formed with the past."

The Rev. Davies announced that the Rev. H. Morgan, Philadelphia, was indisposed and unable to attend. Since its inception the following five ministers had laboured for the movement –

> Rev. David Davies – 3 years; Rev. John Abel – 25 years; Rev. David Griffiths – 2 years; Rev. David Jones – 43 years; Rev. W. C. Jenkins – 52 years; during which period the reverend gentle-

men had established three branches, viz: Sardis, Trimsaran, Soar in Mynydd-y-Garreg, Tabor in Llansaint and Gwendraeth Sunday School.

An admirable address was delivered by Mr Gomer Henry of Llandeilo, touching on memories from the past.

During the service Mr David Davies (Elder official) unveiled a tablet which bore the following inscription in Welsh –

His Holy Temple

To the sacred memory of the late Rev. Evan Davies, Llanedi, and other founders of the cause; also Mr David Jones, Pistyllgwyn, who presented the ground whereon the first chapel was built, it being the first Nonconformist Chapel in the town.

Built 1785, rebuilt 1831, again rebuilt 1873
Removed here in 1926
Sardis (built 1831)
Soar (built 1869)
Tabor (built 1878)
Gwendraeth (built 1890)

Mrs James of Cardiff, daughter of the late minister (the Rev. W. C. Jenkins), unveiled a tablet which bore the inscription –

Servants of God most Highest

In respectful remembrance of the ministers of this Chapel. The Revs. –

David Davies	1787-1790
John Abel	1794-1819
David Griffiths	1820-1822
David Jones	1824-1867
William Castellau Jenkins	1867-1919

The latter, who died March 14th, 1924, at the age of 92 years. An unfeigned man, faithful servant and powerful preacher.

Mrs James also presented an oil painting of her late father to the custody and safe keeping of the church, where he had laboured for 50 years.

Mr James of Neyland (son-in-law of a former minister, the late Rev. David Jones) said that he was most pleased to see so many present, and that everything seemed to be well in favour of carrying on the Christian faith.

Dr Davies, the veteran Newcastle Emlyn minister, gave an address on 'The Works of the Cause' and said that he had preached for 64 years.

Dr Gwylfa Roberts of Llanelly, in his address 'The Church and its Future' rejoiced in the opening of such a beautiful chapel.

The services continued throughout the day, and during the afternoon sessions, the Rev. Dr Davies of Newcastle Emlyn and the Rev. Elvet Lewis, M.A. of London (Archdruid), delivered most eloquent and inspiring sermons.

During the evening services, the Revs. Gwylfa Roberts and Elvet Lewis occupied the pulpit. The number of people who had travelled from various districts for the evening service was so large that an overflow meeting was held at Morfa C.P. Chapel, although the new chapel could hold over 700.

The services continued throughout the week.

11.

People and Places

September 1841 – Commissioners Bridge
A new bridge, potentially hugely advantageous to the community, was constructed over the Gwendraeth Fawr River. When the structure named 'Commissioners Bridge' was completed, an opening ceremony took place at the site located just outside the town on the Kidwelly/ Llanelly route. A good number of people had gathered for the occasion and a marquee had been erected in a nearby field where a plentiful supply of cake and wine had been made available. Later on at the end of formalities, a procession was lined up to take its departure from the site with the booming of ceremonial cannon-fire resounding in the background.

Commissioners Bridge, 2003.
(Photograph: Author).

Town Quay, silted up with mud, 2003.
(Photograph: Author).

1844 – Safe Harbour

Pigots 'Directory of South Wales' records that:

> "Kidwelly Quay is a convenient harbour safe for vessels of 400 tons burden that can come close up to the wharf. The town comes under the jurisdiction of the Dutchy of Lancaster and is governed by a mayor, twelve aldermen and twelve of principal burgesses, assisted by a town clerk and other officers.
>
> Quarter Sessions are held there for trials once a fortnight and a stewards court for small claims is held weekly.
>
> There are places of worship for Baptists, Wesleyans, Methodists and Presbyterians, and the population totals 1,563."

April 1871 – Ewe and Lamb Visit Castle

A ewe and her lamb, the property of H. Anthony, Gardde Farm, succeeded in scaling the height of the loftiest tower in our ancient castle. Pigin Tower is over 150 feet high and the two sheep stationed themselves at the very top, much to the admiration of all who beheld them. Having taken in the impressive and magnificent view, they turned right about face and hoofed their way to the safety of ground level.

May 1872 – Lucky Escape

The handsome spire of St Mary's Church, which measures 180 feet high, had been for some time in a very dilapidated condition. As it was advisable to restore and repair to render it safe, a renowned 'Steeple Jack' and his son were engaged for the purpose. Rev. Tommy Griffiths (Vicar), Mr T. Davies (Mayor) and Mr R. Maliphant (Lay Rector) succeeded in raising the necessary cash to fund the project. With expertise and skillful manipulation, a number of ladders were secured from the walk outside the belfry to safely transcend the summit of the steeple. On the Thursday morning the younger man, 'Steeple John', climbed to the top at a point just below the plain iron cross installed at the apex of the spire, and while applying himself to the task in hand a small piece of the top stone gave way, which could have completely unbalanced him. Fortunately, however, he was able to scramble clear to safety. Bravely he returned to his perilous task, continued with the repair work and stayed there for quite some time. Eventually, he retraced his steps to arrive safe and sound on terra firma. It was anticipated that in a few weeks the spire would be restored to its former glory.

November 1877 – Street Improvements

Steps were taken to improve the antiquated and dangerous pavements in the ancient borough. Repitching with stones would not be much of an improvement and flags, such as had been laid in other towns, would be the ideal solution. Some property owners, such as Dr T. Griffiths of Henblas in Bridge Street, had already upgraded the footpath with flagstones.

1881 – Population Increase

In 1871 the population of Kidwelly numbered 1,830; ten years later in 1881, the number had escalated to 2,231, a 22% increase. Number of houses occupied totalled 445.

April 1881 – Half Day

Efforts by the Rev. W. C. Jenkins, Congregational Minister and Dr Jones, and at the request of some shopkeepers in the area, a decision was made that all shops would close on Wednesdays during the afternoon, thus securing for assistants a weekly half-day holiday.

December 1891 – Stopped Clock

The clock installed on the steeple of St Mary's Church needed to be repaired as it had been out of action since the lightning strike of

1884. Clockmaker, Mr Benson of London, estimated the cost of repairing and providing two extra dials (making four altogether) to be in the region of £60.

July 1892 – Militia

Several numbers of our gallant defenders, members of the Carmarthenshire Militia, made an appearance in the town. They were camped locally, three miles away at St Ishmael's for training purposes.

February 1902 – Peal of Six

The church bells were removed from the steeple and together with the broken bell metal were sent to Messrs Carrs' Bell Foundry at Smethwick, for liquefaction and renewal. Total weight of the old metal amounted to 33½ cwts. The renewed peal of six were to be hung as soon as possible so they would be ready for the celebratory peals on King Edward VII's coronation day. Mr Alfred Stephens volunteered to personally take on the cost of renewing and rehanging the bells which amounted to £135.

October 1902 – Street Numbers

At the Town Council's monthly meeting held on a Tuesday, it was resolved to number all the houses in the town. A decision to provide nameplates in each street had been passed for action at the previous meeting.

March 1914 – Fire

A hayrick, property of James Wild of the Railway Inn at Kidwelly, was discovered to be on fire and most of the hay destroyed, causing a huge loss to the owner.

July 1914 – Lost Well

A delegation of Town Councillors embarked on a search for the lost spring called Ffynnon Diana. The well was discovered without too much difficulty with the assistance of Thomas Nicholas, a veteran of the town who had lived near to the site for many years.

November 1914 – Breakdown

The engine dynamo at Kidwelly Cinema broke down completely one Friday evening, which necessitated all patrons to be reimbursed their admission charge. The cinema remained closed for business on the Saturday following as well.

Pig Fair at Bridge Street. Early 1900s.
(Photograph courtesy Peter Evans).

May 1917 – Live Fowl

Fresh produce and livestock were brought to the Kidwelly Market held at the Town Hall on Saturday. Mrs Hannah Davies of Mynydd-y-Garreg entered several pairs of live fowl which sold for seven shillings and sixpence a pair (today's 37½p). A variety of commodities such as butter and eggs were being sold and an ample choice of rabbits was available.

1921 – Clock Work

The clock attached to the tower of St Mary's Church was restored and in working order again. It had been out of order for quite a while and was repaired by order of the Kidwelly Borough Council who paid the charge for rectifying the fault.

May 1922 – Accident

A nasty accident occurred when Mr E. Edwards, cycling down Pinged Hill, was confronted by a cow. In an attempt to avoid the animal he was thrown straight into the window of a shop owned by Miss J. Rees of Causeway Street. Fortunately, he escaped serious injury, having sustained only a few bruises, but the shop window was completely destroyed.

1922 – Thatched Cottage Fire

A large crowd of people gathered at the scene where one of the town's thatched cottages was found ablaze. Luckily there were many willing hands ready and eager to pass buckets of water to extinguish the flames, and soon the fire was under control. Two young ladies ran for the so-called fire brigade, which proved to be a futile exercise anyway, as the firefighting equipment was long out of repair. A potential disaster was avoided but the roof unfortunately was burnt out.

1927 – Fair Nights

The Council ordered that in future the lamps in Station Road, Bridge Street and Causeway Street remain lit until 11.30 p.m. each night when the Fair was resident in the town.

December 1936 – Trussed Goose

On a Monday in December the Annual Christmas Show of fatstock, poultry, root crops, etc., took place in the grounds of the Kidwelly Mart. There was a good attendance and excellent entries with classes of trussed goose, pair of trussed fowl, dozen eggs, six round potatoes and six kidney potatoes, etc.

1937 – Telephone Kiosk
Summoning help in an emergency of any kind in Mynydd-y-Garreg was only available at a telephone kiosk located in Kidwelly approximately two miles away, and was the reason for a complaint passed to Kidwelly Town Council. The officials failed to reach an agreement even after prolonged discussion and the motion was 'tabled', mainly due to the charge of £4 per year for five years to be met from the Council's coffers.

November 1938 – Early Closing
Grocery retailers met at the Social Club where it was decided that in future local grocery shops would close at 8 p.m. instead of 9 p.m. on Saturday nights. Mr Gerrard Jones of Gwendraeth Stores presided at the meeting and the motion was proposed by D. Beynon Jones of Pinged Hill Stores and seconded by Gough Davies of London House.

March 1939 – Special Award
Sgt. Griff Hughes of Gwendraeth Town, was a long-standing member of St John's Ambulance. He was recipient of a special award and was presented with the Royal Humane Parchment encased in a beautiful oak frame, in recognition of his competence in saving a young lad from drowning at the Bertwn during the previous summer.

March 1940 – War Comforts
The War Comforts Committee at Kidwelly were active in supporting local boys serving the country in HM Forces. House-to-house collections were made each week, and a collection box was established near the Town Hall to encourage either donations of money or cigarettes. Various women's organisations met at allocated places in the town and produced knitted woollen garments of all kinds, e.g. balaclavas, gloves, socks, etc., etc.

December 1941 – Prisoner of War Fund
A Grand Dance was held in the Town Hall in aid of the Red Cross and St John's Ambulance Prisoner of War Fund. Music was provided by the Adelpheans of Burry Port and MCs were Mr P. Squire of Kymers Villa and Dr Beynon Davies of Llys Meddyg.

Kidwelly War Services Comforts Committee.

Chairman :	Treasurer :	Secretary :	Gift Secretary :
J. AMOS JONES, Esq., C.C.	Councillor T. J. SMITH.	D. I. EVANS, Esq.	Miss H. M. THOMAS,
Lakefield Place, Kidwelly.	Amgoed, Kidwelly.	Cefn Parc, Kidwelly.	Penbryn, Alstred Street, Kidwelly.

February 26ᵗ 1946.

Dear Friend,

After over six years continuous service, the Kidwelly Comforts and Welcome Home Committee is now in a position to wind up its accounts and allocate to each serviceman and woman, his or her share of the Welcome Home Fund.

Throughout the duration we have endeavoured at all times to consider the best interests of you all, and believe, from letters received from all fronts, that we have to a great extent succeeded. This feeling of something done, amply repays us for every effort expended, but at the same time, we fully realise that you have had no more than you deserve. Indeed, we only wish we could have done more for you.

The share-out of the Welcome Home Fund has been allocated as follows :—

To every serving man or woman with over twelve months service—£5.
To every person with less than twelve months service—£1 5s. 0d.

This gift is given you as a small token of appreciation from the Townspeople of Kidwelly, who have contributed generously to the Comforts and Welcome Home Fund over a long period.

To those of you who have already returned to your homes, we wish good luck and a bright future.

To you who are still in the services, we would say that your return is eagerly awaited.

We hope that the future holds for you a more promising outlook than has been the case in our Borough for very many years.

We cannot let this opportunity pass without thinking of those who have made the supreme sacrifice, and extend to those they have left behind, our deepest sympathy in their loss.

After these gifts are dispersed, there will be a balance in the Welcome Home Fund of approximately £50. It has been suggested in a committee meeting that this amount be retained until such time as a hall will be erected in the Borough, and that this amount shall form the nucleus of a fund to erect a tablet to those who have given their lives.

If you are in favour of this suggestion will you please indicate your approval on the attached receipt.

The following figures are included as we believe they will be of interest to you.

	£	s.	d.
Revenue from Dances	2,432	19	10
Revenue from Whist Drives	138	14	0
Revenue from Concerts	356	4	11
Street Collections	1,412	14	3
Private Donations	172	13	5
Mynyddygarreg Welfare Committee ...	418	5	6
Bank Interest	22	8	2
Total from all Sources ...	£4,954	0	1

Cash gifts to the value of £2,731 4s. 0d. have already been paid, £292 7s. 8d. was expended on wool for garments, while the total of the Welcome Home Fund stands at £1,897 6s. 4d.

These figures are not intended as a Balance Sheet, but only to give you an indication of the sources of revenue, and the amount available for distribution.

With sincere wishes for your future happiness and prosperity,

Yours sincerely,

For and on behalf of the Committee,

J. Amos Jones

Chairman.

(Courtesy Miss Mair Rowlands).

June 1949 – Long Haul

Although Kansas in the USA is 9,000 miles away from Great Britain, American Serviceman GI John Lambuck flew in on a journey that had taken him 11 hours to complete. John had been stationed at

Broomhill during World War II and had made many friends in Kidwelly. He decided to return for a holiday and stayed at the Bell Inn which was run by Cllr. George Gilbert, and where he had spent many happy hours.

November 1963 – Law Courts
The Magistrates Courts continued to be held at the Town Hall in Kidwelly, a distance of 10 miles away from Llanelly where a new badly needed courthouse was under construction.

There were regular courts on Mondays and Wednesdays, a domestic court on Tuesday's and a juvenile court on Thursday's. Chairman, Cllr. D. D. Williams, referred to the inconvenience of travelling to Kidwelly; on the other hand, local business people were very pleased with the extra trade generated by the assiduous functions of legal matters.

Town Hall, 2003.
(Photograph: Author).

12

Horse Racing Dynasty

THREE TIMES GRAND NATIONAL WINNER

When John Anthony of Gardde Farm, Water Street, Kidwelly, married Elizabeth Anthony of Brynmorfa, Tycoch, Kidwelly, in the late 19th century, and set up home in Cilfeithy Farm a few miles from the town, little did they realise they would also set up a horse racing dynasty. John Anthony became well-known throughout the country for the famous horse breeding and training establishment at Cilfeithy Farm and regularly supplied horses to the military forces.

The marriage of John and Elizabeth Anthony was blessed with twelve children – seven boys and five girls. All were eventually to become very much at home in the saddle, having been raised in an equestrian environment. Even their son Gwyn, who was born with a club foot, was equal to any of his siblings on horseback. With such a background it was not surprising that three of the boys, namely Jack, Ivor and Owen became very successful jockeys and hugely successful trainers, finding fame and fortune in the racing world.

The Anthony brothers – Owen, Ivor and Jack – sons of a Welsh yeoman farmer,
who have made racing history as trainers and as jockeys.
(Photograph courtesy Mr Neville Jones).

*Thrice winner of the Grand National (on 'Glenside', 1911, 'Ally Sloper', 1915,
and 'Troytown', 1920) as an amateur, Mr Jack Anthony is pictured with proud
possessions: oil painting of himself on 'Troytown', small cups for other National
wins and the other in the middle presented to him for training
'Easter Hero', winner of the Cheltenham Gold Cup.*
(Photograph courtesy Mr Neville Jones).

Jack Anthony

John Randolph Anthony (Jack) was the more successful jockey who
became a legendary figure in the racing community. Winning the
renowned Grand National, the greatest steeplechase in the world
(an epic endurance test run over 4½ miles) not once but an incredible
three times was indeed an outstanding achievement.

Jack, like his brothers, started his riding career in his father's
hunting stables and began competitive racing in point-to-point
meetings in Carmarthenshire and Pembrokeshire. He won his first
steeplechase at the tender age of 16 years (under National Hunt Rules
at Ludlow in 1906) and went on to become the idol of the steeplechasing world. His three National winners were Glenside in 1911,
Ally Sloper in 1915 and Troytown in 1920. He also finished second,
twice on Old Tay Bridge in 1925 and 1926, and came third on Bright
Boy in 1927. He was in the frame as they say in horse racing circles,
(i.e. to finish in the first three places) six times in the National. My
research revealed that he only ever rode in twelve Grand National
races, and to finish in the first three over the arduous Liverpool course
an impressive six times is an amazing feat of horse riding. Jack
Anthony was fearless over hurdles and at his best over fences,
especially at Aintree – he was a great Aintree Jockey.

The Grand National was, and is still, by far the most important, affluent and lucrative race in the steeplechasing calendar. In the days when Jack was a competitor the fences were extremely harsh and to even finish the course was an heroic accomplishment.

In 1911 Jack gained his first National win when he rode Glenside, a horse with impaired vision; he could see with the left eye only, therefore the horse could only compete at left handed racecourses, such as at Aintree. The young amateur rider, who was a late choice for the race, coaxed the animal over formidable obstacles around a rain-soaked course in appalling conditions, to an epic victory that was rightly acclaimed a remarkable feat of horsemanship.

Jack retired from steeplechasing in 1927 and set up and became a highly successful trainer at Letcombe Regis near Wantage in Berkshire. He was very successful as a trainer, especially with Easter Hero, twice a winner of the Cheltenham Gold Cup in successive years – 1929 and 1930. He also won the Champion Hurdle with Brown Tony in 1930. Jack Anthony was quoted as saying "Easter Hero was the best horse I ever knew, the best horse that never won the National."

'Troytown', with Jack Anthony up. Won Grand Steeplechase de Paris,
as a six-year-old, and the Grand National the following year.
(Photograph courtesy Aintree Racecorse Co. Ltd.).

Phlegmatic, shrewd Ivor Anthony, a successful amateur rider, is seen with cups awarded for training two National winners, 'Kellsboro' Jack' and 'Royal Mail', and for training 'Morse Code', Cheltenham Gold Cup winner.
(Photograph courtesy Mr Neville Jones).

Ivor Anthony

Ivor Anthony began his career in local steeplechases and became a very successful amateur rider. His greatest achievements took place at the Welsh Grand National held at Ely Racecourse in Cardiff. He won the race in 1911 on Razor Bill and finished in third place three times.

Later on, he too became a very successful trainer at Wroughton near Marlborough Downs, twice winning the Grand National – in 1933 with Kellsboro' Jack and in 1937 with Royal Mail. The year 1937 was special in that (a) it was a coronation year and (b) Royal Mail winner of the Grand National was owned by Hugh Lloyd Thomas, trained by Ivor Anthony and ridden by Evan Williams. This was the first time that owner, trainer and jockey of a Grand National winner were all Welshmen. You will see in the picture, a china Royal Doulton commemorative mug owned by Neville Jones of Pantycrug, Llandefeilog. Neville came across the mug displayed in pride of place at the White Hart Inn in Llanddarog. The Anthony boys called there regularly when out riding with the fox and hounds. Eventually, with many visits and a vast amount of persuasion, the landlord Mr Voyle sold this memorable trophy to Neville, but only because there was Anthony blood in Neville's veins.

Royal Doulton Commemorative Mug, 1937.
(Photograph courtesy Mr Neville Jones).

Ivor also had great success at Cheltenham, winning the prized Gold Cup twice – in 1938 with Morse Code and in 1941 with Poet Prince and winning the Champion Hurdle with Chenango in 1934. Ivor was the more successful trainer of the three brothers at the Welsh Grand National. He was a triple winner, training Broomlet in 1930, Peddle Ridge in 1933 and Sorley Boy in 1936; he also trained the runner-up twice and came third once.

In 1940 Bogskar won the Grand National, ridden by 20-year-old Mervyn Jones (Ivor Anthony's nephew), who stepped in as a replacement jockey at the last minute. Mervyn, who was staying with Ivor at the time, rose to the occasion with a great victory on his first ride on the challenging Aintree course and looked to have a great future in steeplechasing. His riding career was cut short when he was killed in action during the war, two years after his epic victory.

Owen Anthony, who trained the immortal 'Golden Miller',
with his private secretary, Francis Carter.
(Photograph courtesy Mr Neville Jones).

Owen Anthony

Owen Anthony, like his brothers, began his career in local point-to-point meetings. Among his many successes as a jockey was being runner-up in the Welsh Grand National on Creolin in 1905.

He took out a licence to train in 1921 and is probably best remembered for his training of Golden Miller, winner of steeplechases all over the country. Golden Miller won the coveted Cheltenham Gold Cup a record six times and was trained by Owen on the sixth occasion in 1936. Golden Miller is the only horse to have won the Cheltenham Gold Cup and Grand National in the same year which occurred in 1934, the one and only time he completed the National course. He set up a record time at that race, one he held until it was beaten by the great Red Rum. Owen also trained Roman Hackle, winner of the Gold Cup in 1940. He trained Music Hall, who was victorious in the Grand National in 1922 and won the Champion Hurdle with Solford in 1940. Owen also operated out of Letcombe Regis and the success of the horses he trained made him famous. The majority of the horses were steeplechasers, many being household names in the racing fraternity – Golden Miller, Kilstar, Knight of the Border and many others.

A tale which has been handed down over the years refers to the time when any one of the Anthony boys was entered in a race meeting, either as a jockey or trainer. Their father would want to know how they had fared. In those far off days, the nearest telephone to Cilfeithy Farm was at Llandefeilog Post Office. He would send one of the family, usually Gwyn, who would ride over to phone for the racecourse results. Gwyn was born with a club-foot and had difficulty walking, but on horseback he was equal to the rest of the family. He was also an amateur jockey, but because of his deformity was only allowed to enter local point-to-point races, many of which he won.

When Gwyn learned that the result of the race was good news, he would be on tenterhooks to get back home and tell father. He would take the quickest possible route, making no attempt to follow the road, but travelled as the crow flies in a direct line to Cilfeithy. Across the fields he would take his steed jumping every obstacle in the way, gates, hedgerows, fencing, until he arrived at the farm with the result.

That's what I call real horsemanship.

It was not until 1927 did the B.B.C. broadcast a running commentary of the most important race in the steeplechasing calendar – the renowned Grand National.

Another memory which has been handed down over the years was of the time when all the boys were home together, and all the family would gather round the piano for a good old sing-song – a real Welsh flavoured homecoming.

CHELTENHAM GOLD CUP

Easter Hero won in 1929 and 1930 trained by Jack Anthony.
Golden Miller won six times, the last time (1936) trained by Owen Anthony.
Morse Code won in 1938 trained by Ivor Anthony.
Roman Hackle won in 1940 trained by Owen Anthony.
Poet Prince won in 1941 trained by Ivor Anthony.

GRAND NATIONAL

Glenside won 1911 ridden by Jack Anthony.
Ally Sloper won 1915 ridden by Jack Anthony.

Troytown won 1920 ridden by Jack Anthony.
Music Hall won 1922 trained by Owen Anthony.
Kellsboro' Jack won 1933 trained by Ivor Anthony.
Royal Mail won 1937 trained by Ivor Anthony.

CHAMPION HURDLE CHALLENGE CUP

1928	Brown Jack	won	trained by Ivor Anthony.
1930	Brown Tony	won	trained by Jack Anthony.
1934	Chenango	won	trained by Ivor Anthony.
1940	Solford	won	trained by Owen Anthony.

WELSH GRAND NATIONAL

1905	Creolin	2nd	ridden by Owen Anthony.
1906	Sunstroke	3rd	ridden by Ivor Anthony.
1911	Razorbill	won	ridden by Ivor Anthony.
	Aerosat	3rd	ridden by Jack Anthony.
1914	Simon the Lepper	3rd	ridden by Ivor Anthony.
1921	Gerald	3rd	ridden by Ivor Anthony.
1922	Mythical	3rd	ridden by Jack Anthony.
1925	Old Tay Bridge	2nd	ridden by Jack Anthony.
1930	Broomlet	won	trained by Ivor Anthony.
	Favourite Star	3rd	trained by Ivor Anthony.
1931	Vinicole	2nd	trained by Ivor Anthony.
1933	Pebble Ridge	won	trained by Ivor Anthony.
1936	Sorley Boy	won	trained by Ivor Anthony.
	Free Wheeler	2nd	trained by Ivor Anthony.
	Golden Miller	3rd	trained by Owen Anthony.

The Welsh Grand National was run at Ely Racecourse until it was closed in 1939.

The Anthony brothers have an unrivalled record here as jockeys and trainers. Ivor Anthony was the most successful, riding Razorbill to victory in 1911 and then going on to train three winners in 1930, 1933 and 1936. In 1930 Ivor Anthony trained the winner and the third placed horse, while in 1936 the Anthonies made a clean sweep with Ivor training the winner and runner-up, and brother Owen training the third placed horse.

Bibliography

Scrapbook Greenwood Case, Sir Edward Marlay Samson. November, 1920.
Famous Trials 4 – Greenwood, James H. Hodge, London, 1954.
Greenwood Collection, Llanelly Library.
The Holy Wells of Wales, Francis Jones, Cardiff, 1954.
The History of Seeplechasing, Michael Joseph, London, 1966.
The Welsh Grand National, Brian Lee, Stroud, 2002.
Yr Eglwys yng Nghymru, Eglwys Deoniaeth Cydweli. Llanelli, 1962.

Carmarthen Journal.
Llanelly and County Guardian.
Llanelly News.
Llanelly Mercury.
Llanelly Star.
The Welshman.

Museum of Welsh Life, St Fagan's, Cardiff.
Aintree Racecourse Co. Ltd., Liverpool.